New Day...
New Year...
New Life!

A JOURNEY OF HEALING; FAMILY ALCOHOLISM &
CHILDHOOD INCEST

LINDA KAY

WESTBOW
PRESS®
A DIVISION OF THOMAS NELSON
& ZONDERVAN

This book is a work of non-fiction. Unless otherwise noted, the author and the publisher make no explicit guarantees as to the accuracy of the information contained in this book and in some cases, names of people and places have been altered to protect their privacy.

WestBow Press books may be ordered through booksellers or by contacting:

WestBow Press
A Division of Thomas Nelson & Zondervan
1663 Liberty Drive
Bloomington, IN 47403
www.westbowpress.com
844-714-3454

ISBN: 978-1-6642-9769-2 (sc)
ISBN: 978-1-6642-9771-5 (hc)
ISBN: 978-1-6642-9770-8 (e)

Library of Congress Control Number: 2023907113

Print information available on the last page.

WestBow Press rev. date: 06/15/2023

CONTENTS

LIFE CYCLE OF BUTTERFLY

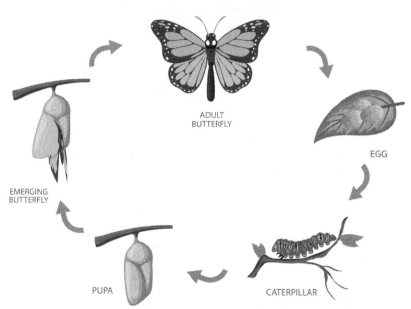

ADULT
BUTTERFLY

EGG

EMERGING
BUTTERFLY

PUPA

CATERPILLAR

INTRODUCTION

The confusion and anger dumped into my life through childhood sexual abuse (incest), beginning at age 12, was like unidentified poison to my soul. This trauma affected my emotional development, and without understanding, I began to live a shame-based life. Shameful thoughts would come into my head like "there must be something wrong with me." As an adult, alone and isolated, it was like I was in an old-fashioned telephone booth with the door closed, and outside the world went on without me. I wanted to belong and to be loved. Outside the booth, people were laughing, and happy families were together living life. I had no idea how to get outside and live. I wanted to scream "just tell me what to do?"

My marriage at age 21 was good at first. Later, due to disappointments and stresses, my husband's drinking increased, and I found myself even more alone and isolated. My confusion increased. I would have obsessive thoughts over and over, such as "how do I live, and what should I do?" Over time, anger grew to rage disguising as self-pity. I had no understanding of my own feelings nor knowledge of how to resolve them. I only knew sadness. Alcoholism got worse in our home, and I struggled. I did not know how to make life better or how to fix it. Looking back, I was full of pride. I didn't know where, how or who to ask for help.

On the cover of this book is a picture of a Monarch Butterfly resting on a Michigan Milkweed. The above drawing depicts the life-cycle of a butterfly. The butterfly begins as an egg, cycles through to

Its' life within the cocoon to begin the struggle to freedom. From the cocoon and hardship of its' struggle, a beautiful creature emerges. As a lover of nature, I relate to the butterfly. I have struggled to become a woman at peace, with purpose for living and healthy self-esteem. Around age 30, I began my struggle, fighting my way out of my cocoon (my telephone booth). I hit an emotional bottom and began the healing journey toward freedom and living.

It is now the desire of my heart, to share my story. My hope is that I write about my healing, in an open and candid way, telling what happened to me, what my life was like then and what life is like now. I want to write and share with the reader from two points; what an imperfect and ordinary human I am, and give enough detail for others, who have been harmed or victimized, to identify with. I pray God will use this book to help others. In the healing process, you might become stuck? A new insight may be needed to move forward. Perhaps, this book will provide a new word, thought or resource that stimulates new insight.

In reading this book, my hope is you encounter something that inspires, empowers, or excites you. Perhaps, you identify in some way and need to take that first step on your healing journey, make a renewed commitment toward healing or share the book with someone you know?

DEDICATION

It is with a full heart of love and gratitude that I dedicate this book to my husband Charlie and daughter Annie. Their love motivated me to face myself, seek help and learn; and it fueled my drive to be a better woman, wife and mother.

Charlie, my husband, who is now deceased, was not a man of many words. In Charlie's process of healing, he found his voice. He had always been a quiet man, but he now would listen intently and quietly. When Charlie felt it necessary to speak, people would listen. I came to value that in our relationship. A lot of honesty and wisdom came from his lips to my ears. When I assumed I knew what he thought, or what he might do, he would often surprise me. Case in point, as I remember and while Charlie was still actively drinking, I attended an Al-Anon meeting. As I listened, people shared about their spouses coming into AA. Time came for me to share, I said "huh, you don't know my husband, he will never come through those front doors." I thought Charlie too proud and stubborn; he surprised and proved me wrong. When he did walk through those doors, months later, he never drank again. Charlie, was the love of my life and inspiration to me. I watched as he fought to gain control over drinking and gained strength through faith in God. He showed such gratitude for life, and later he showed such grace as he faced Multiple Sclerosis and liver cancer.

Annie, my daughter and "miracle child", inspired me from the moment of her birth. Annie inspired me to work and strive to be the best Mom possible. I wanted to be a woman she could be proud of. I know all moms probably feel this way, but truly, Annie is absolutely beautiful and perfect, as a baby and now a woman. Enjoying her as a beautiful baby and watching you grow; I witnessed a childhood of innocence and curiosity. As she explored and learned about life and her environment, I too learned. Annie taught me things I hadn't experienced or remembered as a child. Some of my fondest times were reading books to Annie at bedtime. I would observe her little face, laughter and curiosity. Annie, you responded in innocence and honesty from a child's perspective. Today, I could not be more grateful to have the experience of being Annie's mom. Annie is a precious gift from God.

Annie, you are beautiful, independent, intelligent and I love you so very much. I respect you and am proud of you. I applaud your accomplishments and give God thanks for your life. I am proud of the compassionate woman you are. Annie, I dedicate this book to you. Your wisdom and input are treasured, even when we disagree, thank you for honesty!

RECOGNITION AND THANKS

Thanks to all those many people who encouraged and helped me on this journey. You shared experiences, understanding and knowledge with me.

At different times in my life, I connected with people through organizations I was involved in. Organizations such as Open Hearts Ministry, AA, Al-Anon, and non-denominational and Lutheran churches. These people talked with me, listened to me and answered my questions. I was challenged to dig deeper into my past, my feelings, and look at what I believed or valued. I began trusting and sharing my deepest thoughts and pain. I felt heard and was responded to without judgement. I truly was loved unconditionally.

Special thanks to three women who were the first to encourage me in writing my story. These women were the first persons to read my beginning and give me feedback. Through periods of procrastination and doubt, these women have encouraged, supported and prayed for me. One of them, Sharon who was a dear kind soul, was sick with the COVID virus and passed away. Donna, Mary and I miss Sharon in our group; which we labeled as the "Traveling Sisters" on our adventures together. As traveling sisters, we would pray on our adventures that God would bring the people to us that we might pray for. As a result, we met a lot of interesting people in our travels who would open up and share harsh or happy circumstances. We listened and, if they were receptive, we would pray with them on the spot. Donna and Mary, these memories will continue to sustain us in our faith that God loves and is present always.

Donna and Mary, you are kind, loving, faithful and fun women of God. You continue to pray for me and teach me about relationship with God, how to love others and how to play. As you know, we have prayed, cried and laughed together. I am so grateful for your friendship, your love, your prayers and your inspiration. Thank you from the bottom of my heart.

Another person I must thank is Rick Roman, Donna's husband. Rick, you encouraged me and I thank you so much!

Author, Linda Kay

CHAPTER I

A Journey of Healing; Walking through Childhood Incest and Alcoholism

Friday, a new day and year has dawned. It is the first day of 2021. Due to the COVID-19 virus, Michigan's Department of Health mediation restriction has shut things down and asked us to travel only if urgent, to stay at home and not gather in homes or other places. This is definitely an unusual beginning to a new year. Here I am, alone at home with no plans to gather in celebration with family and friends. Restaurants are closed to dining-in, movie theaters and many entertainment places, and churches are closed.

I slowly enter the day wondering "how do I spend my 2021 New Year Day? It certainly is not like any other new year day. Spending time to make all those usual new year resolutions didn't seem necessary, since I never seem to keep or stay consistent in following my resolutions. So, my decision is to be quiet and be internally reflective, a day with me living through one moment at a time with God. I begin stretching and exercising my body. Next, I prayed, read my Bible and meditated on the reading and resulting thoughts.

Now, I decide to listen to music and turned on the radio to a Christian radio station. I just caught the ending of a speaker, whom I didn't recognize. The speaker was in the process of closing with prayer. As I listened to the prayer; one sentence lit up my mind like a bright light bulb. This sentence immediately struck my heart with such gratitude; "thank you, God, for turning our scars into our story." I began to weep for joy!

I believe God's small still voice spoke to me in that prayer ending. Those words confirm for me that I am accepted, loved and free from the fears of rejection, abandonment and negative emotions of my past. It is clear, I am here on this first day of 2021 in a Pandemic grateful and experiencing real joy. Instead, I could still be a bitter, resentful, confused, lonely and full of confusion and negative emotions, lost! I had been a woman without a clear set of values, beliefs or personal identity and wondering "what is wrong with me?" or thinking "Nobody loves me and how do I fix me?" Thoughts like these permeated a large part of my adult life; along with a deep sense of never measuring up, unworthiness and obsessive thinking trying to figure it all out. In the past, I had So often thought, "I just wish someone would tell me what to do, how do I become normal?"

Before beginning my journey to heal, the picture of my life would be like an old-fashion red telephone booth. I would be inside the booth with the door closed and looking out at people living life. These people outside the booth, looked like they were living life. They were laughing, talking, holding hands but paid no attention to me in the booth. I could not figure out how to get outside to join and be part of life with them. I wanted to join them but had no clue. This is the picture I would use to describe my life before healing.

On this new day and new year, I had heard the ending sentence of the prayer and in my thoughts, it was clear to me. I knew in this moment of my life, here and now in a 2021 Pandemic, my emotional woundedness no longer dominated my mind nor controlled my life. My scars had been turned into "my story". My crying was composed of tears of joy and gratitude flowing from a grateful and humbled heart!

God took my brokenness, healed my emotions and renewed my mind. I no longer walk around in a state of confusion about my identity or self-worth. I am clear about my identity, belief and faith in God. In the beginning of this healing journey, I had not understood how to process feelings and was emotionally immature. I had just kept doing the same things over and over expecting it always to be better next time. Even though I was hurting and confused, this had become my normal. To me, it felt safer to just keep going on in the same way.

After hitting my emotional bottom and got help, I began to understand feelings, such as anger which stemmed from my fears, I was very fearful. My choices and decisions were not made from a healthy emotional state of mind. Choices and decisions were made from my pent-up emotions, which were often immature and coming from that wounded little girl (Lynnie) inside me. I had a gut load of self-pity, fear of abandonment and much pent-up anger and resentment. These feelings had accumulated and built up inside me for many years. I had held onto my secrets and the dysfunction of my past.

Today, beginning 2021, I have acknowledged much healing and resolution of the past. I am confident in the woman I have become and look forward to continued growth mentally, emotionally and spiritually.

What do I do with this fresh understanding and the joy and gratitude I feel? The thoughts that come and the decision I make is, "to tell my story with the hopes and prayers that it will encourage others who may be struggling with emotional, mental, sexual or physical woundedness from their past." Perhaps my sharing might help someone, who is stuck in a rut of trying to figure it all out on their own. Maybe someone out there feels like nothing ever changes. Perhaps there are some who continue to maintain secrets. Secrets support dysfunction and unhealthy relationships. Someone out there may feel lonely and isolated like I did; locked up in a phone booth with no knowledge of how to get out and live? There are those who still feel worthless and keep trying to please everyone. Sometimes, like me, people may feel responsible for the happiness of others and always blame themselves when things go wrong. For all circumstances, perhaps there is something in my story which will open a door of understanding. I ask myself, "could my story be like the speaker's prayer and touch someone's heart in a way that brings them new insight, gratitude and or joy? I sure pray and hope so."

Maybe there will be some words or information within this book that reaches someone who is ready to give up because they are in such pain and see no hope for their life. Perhaps someone who has tried a lot of positive or negative things to cope, maybe even been in counseling for years and still feels like such a failure or loser. In writing this book, I have the opportunity to encourage others to look at their life and believe. Life can be better and everyone is valuable. Each person born with unique purpose in living. Not sure where you might be on the subject of God? Human beings are wholistic beings with mental, physical, emotional and spiritual needs. I encourage you to ponder your belief or lack of belief in God as you move forward. I did not have a relationship with God when I began my journey. I was angry with God and not clear about what I believed. God will meet you wherever you are, begin with getting help and being true to yourself. I know God will bless those efforts and DON'T give up but keep going "one day at a time."

Thoughts of telling my story, and the desire to help others, were not new thoughts to me. I had felt nudges or promptings to write my story before my husband died in 2015. However, those thoughts became stronger after he died. I had begun to write, multiple times, but would end up not finishing or starting over. I would become overwhelmed with the details of my life. The purpose of writing the story was not clear to me. At times, I felt sort of rebellious or ridiculous thinking I could do it. Sometimes, I procrastinated and avoided making a commitment to the process. Negative thinking would begin in my mind, such as "I am not a writer.", "who would want to read it?' Fears, of rejection and abandonment, would rear their ugly heads. I would continue to procrastinate or avoid.

Today, this new day, the purpose for writing becomes clear to me. I am to write and share my story, as I am convinced, this urging that continues to come back to me is God's spirit within me. Today, I commit and step out on faith, with renewed confidence. I will leave the results of the effort in God's hands. Now, I feel freer to write the book, that continues to nudge my mind. Instead of allowing myself to get caught up in the questioning of purpose or getting bogged down in the details, my mind is free to write the book God desires written.

CHAPTER II

Where to Begin? What Happened?

Where do I begin? I have now lived 76 years, and there is a lot of stories to share. To tell you everything would take volumes. Life is a journey and each day is a new opportunity to live and learn.

Looking back to find a starting point, I begin by focusing on two traumatizing events from my past. The first event, began in childhood (incestuous sexual abuse), which I believe stunted my emotional and mental development. The second event was alcoholism, which became progressively worse over a period of 10 years into my marriage. Recognition of the reality of my struggles and pain took me beyond my denial, and moved me toward healing.

What happened? I was 30-31 years of age. Being married for about ten years, I had arrived at a place where I could no longer repress my pent-up emotions. One example, I would be standing at my kitchen sink to wash dishes and I would begin to cry. I had no idea, or reason I could understand, for the crying. An anxiousness would rise up in me, and I would feel like something inside was going to burst. My inclination was to physically run as hard as I could. But I didn't run, instead I worked more and more. My Friday nights were spent on the sofa watching TV, eating too much and gaining weight. I did not know what was wrong with me. As a person who was such a people pleaser, I would do things for other family members or acquaintances without thought of my own needs. I could not say no. When does one say no to another person? I certainly did not know the answer to that question. My thought was, obviously and surely if I say no, they won't like me and I would be a selfish person. Obsessively, I second-guess myself and would replay in my mind circumstances and conversations involving other people. Had I done or said the right thing? What must they think of me, of Charlie or of our family? I felt like everything negative that happened, or if a loved one was unhappy, it was all my fault and my responsibility to fix it. Of course, these thoughts took place inside me. I concluded that something must be wrong with me, or I must be defective. Maybe something is wrong with my brain? I had no idea what to do or how to help myself.

I had a choice to make. I could continue as I was, or I could stand up for me, get honest with myself, get professional help and take a risk to do whatever is necessary to change my life. After I got help, I came to understand. Emotional and psychological wounds never heal or get resolved without risking and help. Healing of mind, body and spirit is necessary and wholistic. I needed to learn, understand and grow in all those aspects of my person. I had become willing and humbled, acknowledging I needed help. As you read my story, please look for what you might relate to but DO NOT compare yourself with me or anyone else. When we compare ourselves to others, I found I always ended up thinking they are better than me or worse. That thinking would lead me to judging others, instead of learning about them and how we might help one another. The feeling from comparing to others, always made me feel inferior (worthless/different) or superior (prideful in thinking "at least I am not that bad".) Simply, find what helps you. You are in control of you (other people do not control you and you don't control them) and YOU always have a choice.

My healing began with my getting honest about my deteriorating marriage, and my spouse's excessive drinking. This revelation brought me, by God's grace, to the point of facing my fear. The fear of remaining in my confusion and emotional pain the rest of my life, became greater than my fear of stepping outside myself to risk something different. It was years later, when I began to heal from the second traumatizing event, my childhood sexual abuse by my father, and having way too much responsibility as a child.

CHAPTER III
Marriage and Alcoholism

Around the tenth year of my marriage, my husband's drinking had gotten progressively worse year-by-year. New Year's Eve 1977; I was tired and was having a hard time getting sleep. Charlie had been drinking Christmas Eve and continued, mostly drunk, throughout the holidays. We had gone to Christmas Eve at his brother's home and celebrated with his family, as was the annual tradition. Christmas day we joined my family's holiday celebrations and Charlie continued to drink alcohol beverages. Christmas Day 1977, I became so uninterested and sad. I ended celebrations early and took Charlie and went home. The celebrations had become so lonely for me and were no longer fun. I was tired, alone and was hiding my thoughts and problems from my family members. I didn't think they would understand. Worse, I feared some would talk about me behind my back. When Charlie was drunk or drinking, I could not sleep. Charlie smoked cigarettes. I couldn't go to sleep until he passed out. I knew, if he was sleeping or passed out, he would not smoke. I was afraid he would drop a cigarette and start a fire. We already had burn marks on our bedroom floor.

This new year, 1977, was different for me than past holidays. I had reached, what AA labels "the bottom" when one gets sick and tired of being sick and tired. In other words, doing the same thing over and over with expectations of different results. I had reached my bottom. I was feeling "sick & tired" of the repeat of holidays, which felt less and less like a celebration and without meaning. It was now, a predictable scene, which would end the same, going home with a drunk and feeling so alone. However, I noticed a new thought this new year. The thought "I don't want to live this way for the rest of my life." I didn't understand pride in my life. Looking back, I believe pride had been my only sense of self-worth. It was all about performance, doing the right thing for me. I certainly didn't want people or family members to know or think badly of either Charlie or me. I knew Charlie, other than his drinking, was a really good man. I didn't want them to think badly of him.

I had no close friends to ask for help or support. Realizing now, I could have had close friends, if I had been honest about my life. I was a pleasant person to be around, but I had superficial relationships. While it was not my intent, I was hiding me and was not clear about who I was. I kept myself so isolated. Because I was a performer and looking back, I label that time my "looking good and smelling good period of life". My meaning is, I spent money I didn't have to buy new clothes so I looked good in my clothing and had good personal hygiene. I was very tidy about myself, getting my hair done often and using good smelling products. I always tried to do and say the right thing. I would do things for others that were not sincere, because "the good girl" does everything for everyone and never asks for or needs anything. I took over responsibilities for my husband and other family members, responsibilities I now know belonged to them.

What did I do this new year that was different? I decided to I call the 24-hour hotline for Alcohol Anonymous. A sweet voice answered the phone "AA, Ginny speaking." I told her my husband was drunk in bed and, as I cried, I told her my situation. She calmly listened, and kindly told me about Al-Anon and meeting locations. Ginny said, "there is a New Year's Eve party tonight and I suggest you put your husband in God's hands and go." She advised the party was at a local high school gym and gave me directions. I thanked her and hung up the phone. The thought came, "my life is falling apart and she wants me to go to a party, isn't that ridiculous?" However, the next thought came, "this is not working what do I have to lose?" As I looked back, I know it was God urging me to look past the fear, and I was motivated to take the risk and go. I didn't have a personal relationship at that point with God. I really didn't know what it meant to be in a relationship with God. Certainly, I had no understanding of how God directs me through the Holy Spirit. That thought, of going to the party, was God's grace reaching out to me in my misery and providing the courage to step out of my fear and go to the party.

When I walked out of my house to go to the New Year's Eve party, I left Charlie in the house drinking and drunk. He didn't even question my leaving. I had to let go of the fear of him burning the house down. I had stood guard long enough, I had to let go and do it differently this time. I arrived at the high school gym and was met by a married couple (one AA and one Al-Anon), Bill and Betty. They welcomed me and introduced me to people, whom I sat with for the evening. I looked around that gym. There were couples and singles. Adult men and women; of different ages, weight & height, and race. I began to observe. People were laughing, singing, dancing, eating and having fun without alcohol. At midnight, everyone got into a circle around the gym. Everyone held hands and recited the Lord's Prayer, [2]"Our Father who art in heaven etc." I went home that night with a little less weight on my shoulders, thanks to Ginny. I believe God helped me that night to begin my healing journey.

Whatever stirred within me at that new year's party motivated me to desire more of it. The following week, I began attending Al-Anon meetings. I attended meetings regularly and several times a week. I learned so much in Al-Anon. The programs of AA and Al-Anon do not talk about Christianity or Jesus within meetings. As we shared in the meetings, we did talk about a higher power or God as we each understood God. AA and Al-Anon are spiritual programs not religious. I observed, as was true for me, eventually each individual finds their way to or back to God.

It was approximately six months, after I began Al-Anon, Charlie had a bad drinking episode. Charlie had been trying to stay sober. He was very curious, but also not pleased, about me going to those Al-Anon meetings. Charlie woke up with a very bad hangover; and he asked me to go buy him some beer. In AL-Anon, I was learning how I enabled Charlie's drinking and contributed to the problem. I learned from reading daily meditations from my "One Day at A Time" book, and from listening to others' experiences at Al-Anon meetings.

I did some pretty mean things to try and control the drinking problem. My efforts and actions were to fix Charlie and our marriage. In an effort to control Charlie's drinking, I would be kind and thoughtful after a hangover (kill them with kindness so to speak.) That didn't work, so next time it happened I would be angry, yelling, banging pots, slamming doors; basically, anything and everything to change the drinking. One night we were driving home from my parents' house and Charlie had been drinking. I felt like I was going to burst, so I asked Charlie to pull into a community park. Before Charlie completely stopped, I jumped out of the car and began to run so hard. I couldn't see where I was going, as it was nighttime. To this day, I don't know why I didn't fall or how far I ran. It felt like my heart was going to jump out of my chest. I don't remember to this day how I got back in the car. Looking back, that certainly was not rational behavior, "why was I riding with him while drinking?"

I became obsessed with fixing the problem. Each morning while driving to work, I would practice what to say to him that evening. I thought "if I say the right words, make the right points, then surely he would see or understand what he was doing to himself, to me and our marriage." In the evening, I would begin the conversation I had rehearsed in my head. Within minutes, I would become so angry, yelling and I was definitely the one emotionally out of control.

Alcoholism is a family disease. I thought Charlie was the problem and he thought I was the problem. He didn't try to fix me; he just used my behavior as an excuse to drink and numb his pain. Following drinking episodes, I wanted to believe him, I would believe him over and over that next time would be different. Charlie would be remorseful and assure me he would change. Neither of us was getting any help or talking to anyone, we just got on this merry-go-round that was predictable after every drinking episode. With no change in the household, the stage was set for the next episode.

Repeatedly, we would go over to my parent's house on the weekend. My dad and others would play music and beer and liquor was always available. Charlie would promise me, this time, he would not drink so much. Each time I believed him. He may have meant it. With alcoholism, he took one drink and he was out of control and would take another. One Friday night, while driving us home, he was really drunk. As I drove, I was getting angrier every time I looked over at him. His head was bobbing around. Exiting the expressway, there was a stop light at the end of the ramp and we had a red light. I neared the red light and I slammed on the brakes so hard, so I would throw him forward to hit his head. I wanted to hurt him the way he was hurting me. Thank God for seat belts, he didn't hit the glass. When I write this, I truly wish I could take that back. I loved him. My behavior was mean. People with unresolved hurt and pain will hurt others.

I did all those things to impact and control his drinking. But, this hangover day, I told Charlie "No" I would no longer buy him alcohol. He was so mad at me and so very sick. There was no confusion in me, I knew I had to say "no "and stop enabling or trying to control his drinking. The drinking was his problem, not mine. Charlie was too sick to go buy beer himself, so he toughed it out. I had begun turning Charlie over to the higher power and letting go. Charlie's drinking was no longer my problem to solve.

Al-Anon taught me to examine my way of thinking. Changing me was within my control. I came to believe I could make significant changes in my life. The only person, on this earth, I can control is me. it was not my responsibility or within my power to stop

Charlie's drinking. This new way of thinking helped me change how I responded to Charlie. Simply, my responsibility is to be responsible for my own actions and emotions, and leave Charlie in the hands of his Higher Power (God as he understood him.)

Since I did not go buy beer and he was too sick, Charlie asked me if I would call the pastor. I had been attending a Lutheran Church. Charlie asked me to call him to see if he would come over and talk with him. I said 'yes", and I called.

Charlie did not know, because of my own distress, I had talked to this pastor about our home circumstances. Pastor responded positively and came to our house. A question Charlie asked was whether he honestly believed in God. Pastor was so honest, non-judgmental and accepting of Charlie. He answered Charlie by saying "I have never seen God but yes, I believe. The pastor confronted the fact that Charlie was sick and said "I think your wife might know some people from AA and Al-Anon who could help." He advised Charlie that AA might be able to help him, and suggested I might be willing to call some people to come over and talk with him. I was unaware, at that time and learned later, pastor had a brother who was alcoholic. So, he was personally familiar with alcoholism and AA. God's grace reached out to us, and sent us his messenger through that pastor.

The first Al-Anon I called was Mary. Mary was so receptive to my call. Mary asked her husband, along with two other married couples, to come to our home that evening. Those in AA met with Charlie in the kitchen, and those in Al-Anon met with me in our living room. I will never forget those couples. For their anonymity and privacy, I cannot name them. Forever, I will love them and be grateful to them. These folks were older than Charlie and I. It was what we needed, as they were rich in years of sobriety, wisdom and experience. From what occurred that night, I did not know how but I knew things were going to change in our home. I heard my husband admit how much and how often he was drinking. He admitted he did have a problem with alcohol. His struggle was worse than what I had known. He had been drinking before going to work on Mondays, following a weekend binge and hangover. Charlie shared he had tried to buy beer on a credit card. Buying anything on credit was so against his personal belief, which was not to use credit cards. Another incident that impacted him, was going to the local Quick Mart to buy beer and was refused. The cashier told him he was already drunk and would not sell it to him. As I look back on these events, I know they were demoralizing to Charlie. As they call it in AA, Charlie had hit his bottom.

It was suggested to Charlie, that evening, he should go into Kent Community Hospital for detoxification. He was hungover and shaking. I drove him to the hospital and they admitted him for detox. It took a week for his system to detox. During the week, he participated in the rehabilitation program by attending one-to-one counseling and AA meetings. When he was discharged from Kent Community, he began attending AA meetings at the Alano Club on College Avenue in Grand Rapids, Michigan.

Charlie never missed AA meetings and went faithfully every night of the week. Together, we attended Saturday night speaker meetings open to both Al-Anon and AA participants. It was called Saturday Night Speaker's Meeting where individuals or couples would share their story. They would tell what it was like when drinking, or living with a drinker; what happened to bring them to AA or Al-Anon; and what their lives were like after AA or Al-Anon. Charlie connected with guys in his meetings. He developed bonds with some who became his very close friends. He had two, Denny and Bill, who were like brothers. Charlie, Denny and Bill, who we called the 3 musketeers, supported each other through many years of AA. They loved and counseled each other, as they maintained their sobriety in AA. Some people have many slips in their sobriety and return to drinking for a while or they never get sober. As far as I know, the 3 musketeers never drank again.

The twelve steps of AA and Al-Anon are applied personally, as each person takes a moral and spiritual inventory of themselves. To paraphrase briefly, step one is accepting our powerlessness; second step is to believe in a power greater than ourselves; and step three to make a decision to turn our lives over to the care of God, as we understood him." These twelve steps are read and discussed in meetings, and each person has opportunity to share their personal experience, along with their strength and hope. These steps, from one to twelve, provide a framework for healing and learning; leading to productive living and better relationships with ourself and others.

Step twelve, "having had a spiritual awakening as the result of these steps, we tried to carry this message to alcoholics and to practice these principles in all our affairs." This step is called the service step, imploring us to carry the message of healing and hope to others struggling. The first year, Charlie in AA and me in Al-Anon, working out our marriage issues was not possible. It was necessary for Charlie to focus on his sobriety, working through those twelve steps and living one day at a time. After work and supper, we both would go to a meeting. The rest of our time, we were learning and healing individually from the effects of living in alcoholism, along with working our jobs and taking care of our house. We basically lived together as roommates. Things had built up and the anger lingered. At times, it was intense and silent in our home. We were not ready or able to work out our marital issues. Healing had to occur individually and we needed to gain knowledge, learn about ourselves and our relationship, and observe to learn from other people in the programs. As we began to practice step twelve and became involved in work serving in chairing meetings, representing our group at regional or state AA and Al-Anon events, our marriage began to be better. We were not lonely any more, nor isolated. Part of our service work was helping new people, as they came to AA or Al-Anon for the first time.

We began to socialize with others. Before a meeting, we would often go out to a restaurant or have coffee or meal with other couple(s). Others in AA and Al-Anon, began to invite us along with other couples into their homes after a Friday or Saturday meeting. We became humbled by occasionally attending a midnight meeting on Saturday night where drunks would come in off the street. As we observed the behavior and appearance of these people struggling, sometimes sober and sometimes not; we were reminded of what we often heard in AA and Al-Anon, "there but for the grace of God go I".

Charlie and I became very close friends with a couple Denny and Bobbi. These two were closer to our age. All four of us had started the programs at about the same time. We would often meet at a 24-hour Big Boy Restaurant. Denny and Bobbi had older children, but Charlie and I didn't have any. We talked about life, our personal and marriage issues. No subject was off the table. We laughed at ourselves and at each other, as we shared. These friends helped us so much.

We extended our service work by becoming regional leaders for our individual group meeting. We would come together with others from AA and Al-Anon groups all over Michigan. At these regional gatherings, there would be separate meetings for AA and Al-Anon. There would be an agenda with any topic affecting our groups, such as funding issues (Al-Anon and AA are self-supporting), group issues, new literature or updated literature used within meetings. It would be our responsibility to serve, which we did by reporting the information back to our group. AA and Al-Anon Conferences were held in Spring and other times within Kent County. There were annual and national conferences held sometimes in Michigan, or another state.

Charlie became a member of the Kent County AA Service which supports a 24-hour hotline for people to call AA. Charlie was on that hotline call list and would answer calls transferred to our home all hours of the night. He would listen to the person on the end of the phone line, who was struggling with alcoholism or were questioning whether or not they were alcoholic. Sometimes he'd come back to bed and say "he or she is not yet ready to quit. Charlie had a list of meeting locations and would give out meeting information. He would know when someone was sincere in acknowledging their problem. Perhaps they were ready for AA, so he would often offer to meet them at the meeting. The worst call for Charlie was when an AA member, sometimes he knew them, had gone back to drinking.

Al-Anon did not yet have a 24-hour answering hotline. As part of my service work, I began working with an Al-Anon committee to establish a 24-hour hotline for Kent County. We did accomplish our goal and established the 24-hour hotline in Kent County.

Connecting with others, and giving back through service work, helped Charlie and I to share, care and understand each other and other people. Serving others through service work, took us to something greater than ourselves and helped heal us.

Charlie never drank again, he stayed sober until he passed away in 2015. He never slipped or went back to drinking, not even once.

Charlie and I had always celebrated with his family on Christmas Eve, as our tradition. After being in AA and Al-Anon for a while, we began a new Christmas Eve tradition for us. We liked walking in Woodland Shopping Mall on Christmas Eve, and would go there a couple hours before going to Christmas Eve celebration. Those few hours, before the mall closed on Christmas Eve, were quieter and not too many people shopping. We enjoyed the Christmas decorations and lights. One Christmas Eve (don't remember the year), Charlie and I came upon a glass blowing demonstration. We watched this artist, who also was selling his glass creations. There were beautiful objects of glass art in different colors, sizes and images. I looked over at Charlie and noticed he had tears in his eyes. He was looking at a white glass cross with a red glass heart in the center of the cross. I was perplexed and thought "why the tears?" Charlie soon enlightened me when he said "I know who freed me." A regret I have is not buying that cross. I know we didn't have a lot of money, but I sure wish to this day I had bought it for him. I was so moved emotionally and I saw the sincerity of his heart and emotion. My love and appreciation for my husband deepened in that moment and continued to grow over the years.

Our marriage never became perfect, but it was good. We loved each other and had lots of joyful moments and much laughter.

When Charlie didn't like something that I did or how I did it, he would bring his frustration to my attention. He would pronounce my name loudly, putting a hard pronunciation on the L and A, like "L...IND...A." I would see his frustration. During my years of unworthiness and taking things way too personally, I would argue back, get mad. In later years of our marriage, those circumstances became a time for smiles and outright laughter at times. I had become comfortable with my humanity. Human beings make mistakes and I am human. Thus, I would not take it personally, but instead, with a very soft and loving voice I would say, "well honey, I am just not as good as you are." It became a joke and a reminder to us both. He would look at me, with his quirky-boyish smile, and say "you got that right". Other times he would smile and say nothing, or he might say "well you are not a Latvian." He was very proud of his Latvian heritage. Frustration would leave him. We smiled at each, or sometimes laughed out loud.

CHAPTER IV

Charlie, My Husband

As the man I got to know and spent 48 years with, my heart desires to share a little background on Charlie's life. Also, to tell how we connected with each other. I would love to have him here with me, so he could share his story himself. Charlie had emotional wounds affecting his life and choices. Alcoholism was the catalyst, which brought him and me to the point of surrender. This book is also about our story, together.

Charlie's story amazes me. His family survived leaving Latvia, living in a displaced persons' camp in Germany for years and travelled by ship across the ocean to Ellis Island, New York. Charlie or Karlis, his Latvian name meaning Charles, was about 2 years old, when His entire family of five (mom, dad, Charlie, older brother and sister) left Latvia by horse and buggy traveling to the Baltic Sea. They boarded a ship to Germany. Charlie's Dad, Janis, knew the Russian Communists were cruel and oppressive. Russian military were entering Latvia and German military were also entering, there would be an obvious clash. Nazis had desires to dominate the world, as they had already taken over many European and Baltic countries surrounding Latvia. Janis had concern for his family. Janis knew Russia or Germany would end up occupying Latvia. Charlie's family arrived in Germany and ended up in the Displaced Persons (DP) camp. Latvians tended to have blonde hair and blue eyes. Germany considered them part of the Aryan Race or master race, which the Nazis' justified as the superior race. Charlie, brother John and sister Velta, suffered through leaving their home and the people and things they cared about. The family could only take a few possessions, along with the clothes they wore. In the DP camp, their mother Elvira was separated for a while due to tuberculosis. Those young kids, I am sure, were fearful. They did not know each day what was happening to her, nor what would happen to all of them. A lot of strain was on the oldest sister to help the family. Charlie told me there were instances of danger and sometimes gun fire around. Charlie and his siblings did not talk or share much about their experiences there in camp.

Germany was defeated and the war ended when Germany surrenders in May 1945. At the end of the war, control for their DP camp was taken over by the United States. In 1949, Charlie's family left Germany and boarded a large ship, General Ballou to travel to U.S. Charlie was about 9 years old. They arrived, with other displaced persons, at Ellis Island, New York.

In order to leave Ellis Island and enter the U.S., immigrants were to have no criminal convictions, each person had to be free of disease, and the family was required to have a sponsor who provided them with a place to work and live. After processing at Ellis Island, the family travelled by train to Greensboro, North Carolina. They were sponsored by the Lutheran Church, through a program supported by Senator Scott of North Carolina. The Scott Family, a prominent dairy farming family, provided work and a place for Charlie's family to live. Charlie's Mom had been trained in Latvia in the care of dairy cows. All members of the family worked on the farm. Charlie, along with his sister and brother, began attending North Carolina public school. They knew very little English. From what Charlie shared with me, it was very hard for him to learn English language, reading and spelling. He was the youngest, so I am sure it even more difficult for his older brother and sister.

I believe it was God's grace that brought Charlie and I together.

As, I was born and lived in North Carolina. Charlie and I actually lived in North Carolina about 96 miles from each other, he in Greensboro and me in Hickory. Both our families moved from N.C. to Michigan when each of us was 15+ years old. We met in Grand Rapids, Michigan through my dad. Charlie had been attending college, but he stopped to work for a while and worked same place as my dad. My dad did upholstery work on the side and Charlie was customizing a baby blue and white 57 Chevy Bel Air. Charlie began coming to our home often, to work with my dad on recovering car seats. Charlie and I dated about 6 months. Since he was not in school, he was drafted into the Army in 1964 during Vietnam War. We wrote letters to each other, and dated when he was home on leave. After basic training in Fort Knox, Kentucky, he was stationed at Fort Sam Houston San Antonio, Texas and educated as a medic. When Charlie came home on leave, he would have a great tan. His blonde hair and blue eyes really stood out from his tan and behind his beautiful smile. He was so handsome and I was definitely infatuated. When he was gone, I missed him. What stood out to me about Charlie was I always felt physically safe with him, he was a thinker, he was a hard worker, educated and he was handsome with a fine car.

Charlie served for two years and was honorably discharged in 1966. Shortly after, he asked me to marry him. On June 10, 1967, a happy but extremely hot day, we were married. As I understood love at that point, I loved Charlie. However, I had an unrealistic idea of marriage and life. My mindset was sort of like a soap opera where everything is wonderful and we lived happily ever after. I gave no thought to how to resolve conflict, or that we would ever have conflict. I was looking forward to buying a house with a white picket fence. Of course, I would have children. A little girl to dress in frilly dresses with black patent baby doll shoes and ruffled lacey socks. A little boy in short pants with little dressy shirts and bows ties. In that time period, the "have it all together families" dressed their kids that way.

Charlie had a lot of unresolved emotions still causing him a lot of hurt and pain. He did not talk with his family about those things, nor did he have the tools for identifying or resolving the wounds. What he experienced during the war in Latvia and Germany, traveling to a new country, crossing the ocean and ending up in a public school system not knowing English. Charlie told me about the embarrassment of reading out loud, and having to learn English while trying to learn subject matter. He had an English teacher that thought him lazy or ignorant just because he was not good at English. Another difficult thing for him, was being a medic at Fort Sam Houston General Hospital, during Vietnam, he was subject to being deployed to Vietnam at any time. Also, seeing others die in the hospital that he provided care for. Charlie did not get deployed and served at Fort Sam for his term in the Army. Along with other young persons in the military during Vietnam, he lived with the uncertainty of deployment. It was an emotional roller coast of being drafted and always being on alert as to whether or not he would go to Vietnam. Charlie had saved the written evaluation reports, which his superiors wrote evaluating his performance. I still have those reports, which indicate Charlie was outstanding in the care he gave and in every way except for one issue consistently. The reports indicate he is too sensitive to ward circumstances. To me, Charlie never wanted to hurt anyone or see anyone hurt. I think it broke his heart every time someone died.

Charlie passed out of this world peacefully. His hurts of life had been healed and scarred over; his scars turned into "his story". I wish he was still here to help me put more of his words into this book. His life was redeemed and his living was purposeful, as he helped many others. In his living and through what he had learned and experienced, he finished high school and two years of community college. He never gave up when disappointed. He faced his struggles with alcoholism and later with Multiple Sclerosis. Throughout his sober period of life, he offered support, helped and encouraged others struggling with their addictions to drugs and/ or alcoholism.

I am grateful I was around for his sobriety. I look upon him with love in my heart and with great respect.

Charlie could have made the choice to continue his life drinking which may have eventually killed him. I don't think our marriage would have survived, if he had not gotten sober. I could not have continued to live with alcoholism in our home. He chose the more difficult choice of facing himself and getting sober, he took responsibility for his actions and he spent time in AA healing his woundedness and helping others. The path to sobriety is difficult and alcohol addiction is strong. Charlie and I both knew others who died from the effects of alcoholism. Alcoholism causes loss of life through an accident while drinking or alcoholics end their own life through suicide. I forever will hold him in the highest regard and am so grateful for our life together. It is my hope that all who knew him, especially those he helped along the way, will remember him. I hope their memories see him as the person who spoke only after deep thought, was not materialistic, cared about others, someone who faced the giants in his life and that he had a great smile. That is the way I remember him today and I give thanks to God for bringing Charlie into my life.

CHAPTER V

Unexpected Miracle

C harlie, now sober about 7 years, our marriage relationship and
home atmosphere was much better. My longing for Charlie to
be sober was realized. Both of us had good friends in AA and Al-
Anon, were growing and maturing individually, and our relationship
was more loving, honest, and forgiving. However, negative thoughts,
feelings, and memories from the past began entering my mind. I was
losing my contentment. Thoughts and questions, such as "Charlie is
sober, I was happy and now WHAT is wrong with me?" Can I not be
satisfied?" These thoughts and feelings bubbling up were connected
to a secret I had hid for many years. Some of the thinking was
familiar, because it had surfaced in my mind before. But I pushed
the thoughts back down and would do that by telling myself, "It was
a long time ago, get over it; or if you tell you are going to destroy the
family." I even had the thought that, "it is my fault, surely I could
have done something."

The secret, I had been sexually abused as a child. The incestuous
sexual abuse began when I was about 12 years of age, and abuse
continued, in some form, throughout my teen years. I never forgot
those memories; they were always there under the surface. I not only
pushed them down, but would minimize them as no longer relevant.
But now, I could no longer hold them back or dismiss them from
my thinking.

From my life and learning experiences, I believe childhood sexual abuse halted my emotional development. As a teenager, I think the abuse and associated emotional blackmail set me up to make immature, dysfunctional choices in my life. Since these memories and thoughts were all inside my head; no one knew except a younger sister. I always felt different, alone and responsible for my abuse. Certainly, no one would believe me or understand. What do I do now?

I was willing to get help, do something but what? Arriving back to the beginning of a painful part of life. Life before I met Charlie, got married and alcoholism. I asked myself, "where do I start?" I knew, from healing in Al-Anon, I could not fix it on my own. No longer did I have to go it alone, there is a High Power and people who will help me. My first step was to tell my Al-Anon sponsor.

A sponsor is someone who has longevity in Al-Anon, practices the 12-steps in their living and participates in service. This person provides a contact to call when troubled or have questions. Basically, a mentor. Good sponsors help you learn how to live; as well as how to work through and apply the 12 steps. The sponsor or mentor provides encouragement, support and correction.

Dottie was my sponsor and I asked her for time to meet together at her home. I was going to share my secret. We agreed upon a time, and I met her at her home. When I began to share what happened to me, my body had an icy cold physical reaction, I began to shake. I was about 36 years old. I had held on to the secret so tightly, hiding from everyone. Not sure I had an expectation of how Dottie might react. I felt disgusting myself and bad, as I said I believed it was my fault. The reaction Dottie gave me was one of compassion, no disgust. She told me it was not my fault. Dottie advised me to consider counseling therapy. She gave me information for help resources. I received God's love and grace through Dottie.

Now that I had opened myself up to dealing with the abuse, I decided to go to the public library and look for books on sexual abuse and incest. Not many books could be found in 1982 on sexual abuse. I did find the book "The Wounded Heart" by Dan Allender. I cannot remember where I heard or saw information about a YWCA program, which stimulated my thoughts and renewed my interest. The information was about a new program at the YWCA for Survivors of Incest. I called but the program was full, and my name was added to a waiting list. They shared with me about the program, which was a state certified therapist who would facilitate a group of women who were survivors of incest. The group would be limited to 12 participants, and meet weekly for twelve weeks. The YWCA did not call me right away so I waited. During the waiting period, I continued to talk with my sponsor. Also, I began sharing with a very close friend in Al-Anon, Joanne. I received support from both women.

While I was waiting for an opening in the therapy group, an event in my life side-tracked my mind. The event was a miracle pregnancy, yes it was a miracle no other explanation. I forgot about sexual abuse and the YWCA group.

Why do I consider my pregnancy a miracle? A little background, beginning three years after marriage and before alcoholism. I began having severe back trouble and went through a year of doctors and efforts to reduce the pain. No clear understanding of what caused the pain. After a year, the orthopedic doctor treating me felt surgery was the only option to define and address the issue. Surgery was performed and I had a bone fusion of L4, L5 lumbar area. The cause he indicates was a lack of bone in my lower back area. This defect caused instability and movement on the nerves causing pain in my lower back. The doctor thought the defect was from a birth, and to stabilize the area, he had to perform the bone fusion. Surgery was long but doctor felt it went well.

Following surgery, I was a month in the hospital. I was released to return home with instructions to remain in a hospital bed for a 3-month rehabilitation. I was allowed, with help, to get out of bed for bathroom visits. My first night home, I began having difficulty breathing. Charlie was concerned. Charlie had been a Medic in the Army. He had a lot of medical knowledge from working in the Army hospital. Charlie called the doctor in the early morning. The doctor had me describe the pain and hardship in breathing, and he told me I may have blood clots in my lungs. He told Charlie he would send an ambulance to bring me back to the hospital. The diagnosis was small blood clots had formed and were located in both my lungs. Due to recent back surgery, the hospital assigned a resident doctor to watch over the healing of my back and a lung specialist for the blood clots. God's grace took care of me, again. My back was collecting fluid which could have caused an infection. For both reasons, I spent another 2 months in the hospital. I was taken home via ambulance, as I could not yet walk. Also, we lived in an upstairs apartment. Arriving at home, I began rehab of 3 months in the hospital bed and taking blood thinning medication. A visiting nurse would stop by regularly to check my blood clotting and back status. As I healed, visits reduced. I did recover and returned to work following a year of medical leave. Thankful, my employer held my job for me. This whole medical diversion put having a child on hold.

Now I was ready to move on. Build our lives together and fulfill the dreams of owning our own home and having a child. Charlie was not eager for me to get pregnant. I assumed he just didn't want children. Years later, I came to understand, my assumption was wrong. It was not that he didn't want children, he was concerned about me. He had stood by powerlessly watching me through back pain, surgery, and the threat to my life by the blood clots. Today I don't make assumptions of anyone, I ask the questions and listen to understand.

*People get hurt though assumption and judgment;
communications are key to any healthy and loving
relationship.*

I began pressing the issue of wanting a child. We kept trying
to get pregnant, but it wasn't happening. A visit to my gynecologist
brought a referral to a fertility specialist. The specialist ordered a
test to determine function of my fallopian tubes. Results indicated
my tubes were totally closed off due to scar tissue. The specialist
advised I would never have children. I was devastated. It seemed no
one I knew, within my extended family, had an infertility problem.
At a follow-up gynecologist visit, I was informed there might be a
possibility of pregnancy. My gynecologist indicated, after he looked
over the test results and read notes from the specialist, he thought
surgery to remove the scarring might help. However, he cautioned,
my best opportunity for pregnancy would be within the first year
following surgery. The scarring could grow back and my chances of
pregnancy would go down after one year. I did not get pregnant in
that first year. In fact, I waited 12 to 15 years longer.

Charlie was sober 7 years. I had prayed over the years for God
to give me a child. When things were bad before sobriety, I prayed
"God I don't want a child in this mess." Now I was willing to accept
that perhaps having a child was not in God's plan for me. I resolved
to enjoy my nieces and nephews. Then one morning I woke up with
a sickness in my stomach. Normally, I would take Pepto Bismol
for an upset stomach and it would take care of it. This time, that
did not work. A few days passed before I realized I was also late
on my monthly menstruation cycle. Thinking I better contact the
gynecologist, but never did I think pregnant. I called and the nurse
made an appointment for me to have a pregnancy test. I was so
excited just to have the test, that showed promise. The anticipation
of results was great, but I had not told Charlie. To my surprise and
surreal feeling, the test was positive. I was pregnant.

Charlie and I had one automobile. He would pick me up from

work each day. I was so excited and my judgement was impaired with my excitement. When and how to tell Charlie? My answer to that question was not wise. Charlie picked me up from work and we were driving home on the Grand Rapids U.S. 131 expressway. I blurted it out and I thought we were going to have a car accident. He maintained control of the car but was speechless.

When we arrived home that day, my disbelief kicked in. I am thinking "is this really a miracle?" I took a Life Magazine book on the reproductive system out of the bookshelves. How could this happen? Surely my tubes are closed off again these many years. The book was on the reproductive system and had diagrams. I saw how small a fallopian tube is. Without a doubt, this is God's gift, a miracle for us.

My childhood trauma was pushed back in my mind. The YWCA group was forgotten about. Charlie and I talked about the baby, would it be a boy or a girl? There were such good times with friends and family. I was almost 38 years old. Over many years I had attended a lot of baby showers. People were excited for us. Many asked to give us a baby shower. We ended up with 5 baby showers. They were all appreciated and fun. One shower was especially fun. Charlie and I had a blast. AA and Al-Anon couples planned a shower for us. There was a game where you dressed a baby-doll, while the husband and wife each used only one hard and worked together to dress the baby-doll. Using diaper pins, putting one hand behind us, we worked together to diaper the doll. We laughed so hard, and enjoyed every minute. If only there had been cell phones, what great pictures we could have shared immediately. I was so happy and after 3 months felt pretty good up to the last month was a little tough. I was happy and we were happy.

Our Annie was born on Easter Sunday, April 3, 1983, in St. Mary's Hospital, a Catholic hospital. She was healthy, had all her fingers and toes. She was perfectly beautiful. My bed faced a cross on the wall and I was grateful. On discharge day, Charlie arrived to pick us up to go home. He had a car seat belted in the back of the car. We were both so cautious with her, and we agreed I would set in the back with Annie. Charlie drove slowly home; being very careful to get us home safe. This little baby girl motivated me from day one to be someone she could respect. I desired more than anything to be a good Mom.

First-time visits from neighbors, family and friends were soon over and now only periodic. We settled in to being a family, with Charlie and I learning how to parent this child. I wanted to stay home with her and not work outside the home. Financially we were not in a position to commit my being home for an indefinite period of time. Charlie supported me in giving it a try for as long as we could. I resigned my job. Since 16, I had worked publicly. Now, I was home with this beautiful child and Charlie was working daily. Other than the year off for medical leave, I had worked outside the home before and after marriage. I am Annie's Mom, Charlie is sober and her dad, and I thought that I would be happy forever.

It took a while to gain my energy back from challenges of delivery. I wanted to do everything right. So, I decided to breast feed Annie. It became difficult to do so. Annie was not getting enough milk, so always hungry. Disappointed, I switched her over to the bottle. She adjusted fairly soon and began sleeping through the night early on.

My energy was not returning, and I began experiencing a heavy tiredness. I would be sitting in a chair feeding Annie and would be fighting not to fall asleep. I didn't know what was happening, I would ask myself "what is wrong with me, I should be the happiest woman in the world." But instead, I was bone tired and full of anxiety. One evening I was feeling especially anxious. Charlie had a friend from AA, Bill, over for coffee. Charlie didn't understand what was going on with me. He knew I was having a hard time. He said to me, "why don't you go over to the mall walk around and get out of the house for a while, I will watch over Annie." I said "ok", and drove over to the mall. I was only there for a short amount of time. I began to feel like everything around me was closing in. Walking quickly, and very disappointed with myself, I left the mall and drove home in tears. I walked into the house crying. Charlie nor Bill could understand why I was back so early and when Charlie asked, I couldn't explain. I cannot remember exact words, but I said to him something like "I can't stand it here and I can't stand it out there." Charlie and Bill looked at each other. They did not know what to say to this crying mess of a woman.

CHAPTER VI

Childhood Sexual Abuse

B oth good and troublesome memories, thoughts and feelings were coming back to me. Experiences of growing up in rural North Carolina, and the sexual abuse beginning around age 12. When I was 15 ½ years old, my parents moved us to Michigan. Remembering and thinking brought back the circumstances surrounding the sexual abuse, which continued in Michigan. Such memories and thoughts had entered my mind many times over the years, however, I would dismiss them by rationalizing them away. I would avoid and push thoughts, memories and feelings down inside. I had many fears. Fear of abandonment, rejection and ruining my family were immobilizing fears. These fears played out in my mind with thoughts such as "what would people think of me", "how could I destroy my family", "my family would blame me, hate me", and "I should have done something, it's me that is responsible".

Lots of feelings, I didn't understand, were surfacing. A new fear took shape. The fearful thought was "I had not been protected by my mom as a child, how could I know if I would be strong enough to protect my daughter?" I treasured my daughter, dearly loved her, and wanted to keep her safe. The alcoholism had been confronted in our home and Charlie was now alcohol free for eight years. Yet here I am again, unhappy, confused, sad and anxious. I did not feel strong enough to protect Annie. I was afraid of Charlie, or any man, being alone with her. I did not know what to do. So, I turned again to rationalization, telling myself "You have every reason to be happy and should not be feeling like this, get over it!"

I was experiencing a heavy tiredness, and would fall asleep easily. When I sat down to feed Annie, I had to watch myself and make effort not to fall asleep. I was so afraid; I would drop her. My closest Al-Anon friend and Annie's Godmother, Joann, I would talk to and tell her what I was experiencing. Joann would call, or stop by, and I would tell her how tired I was and my fears. The feedback I received wasn't helpful. Joann, and others, would say things like "well you know you are having your first child at an older age", or "give yourself time for your hormones to get balanced." Charlie couldn't help me either, as this was perplexing to him. It was clear I needed to do something, but "what?"

One day while home with Annie, I received a call from the YWCA, the therapy group for Survivors of Incest program. I had put my name on the waiting list for that program before my pregnancy. There was an opening in the program and the caller asked, "would I still like to come?" It was like a breath of fresh air; this was the help I needed. I didn't hesitate I said "yes I would like to join a group." I did continue my Al-Anon meetings at night, along with attending one day a week the group meeting at the YWCA. The nursery, at the YWCA, took care of Annie while I was in group. Charlie did not understand my need to go to the group meeting about incest. However, he never stood in my way.

After the first few sessions, I gained understanding. The tiredness, stress, sadness and anxiety were from repressing and holding onto that secret within myself. I began to learn I was not alone, in that childhood sexual abuse happened to others. Further, there tends to be a dysfunctional family pattern or pathology to sexual abuse. If the secret isn't exposed and the effects dealt with, harm can continue through a family for generations. The behavior needs to be addressed and changed, so the family and those harmed can heal.

It took several sessions in the group, for me and others, to build trust and talk about what happened to each of us. Holding on to my secret was like keeping my feelings and thoughts in a safe; a safe deep inside me with no combination. The more I listened and talked, the freer I felt. I began to learn the combination to my safe, and began to understand my thoughts and feelings. My coping was to numb my feelings, tighten up and just get through it. I had drawn inaccurate conclusions about myself and other relationships. Yes, going to this group was where I needed to be. Understanding grew, and I was renewing my mind. I now had the courage to face my fears connected with the abuse. Here again at a new bottom in my life, God's grace and presence in my life led me. God reached out through the call from the YWCA. God's spirit pursued me to understanding and healing.

Feeling stronger as I learned and healed, I could look at many aspects of my life and see the good things. I was encouraged by the positive memories and thoughts I recaptured. Growing up in North Carolina gave me some of the most fun and happy days of childhood. We were poor and lived in a home, which for several years, was only two rooms. Eventually, there was an addition in a two-bedroom home with me sharing a room with my siblings. We had two sets of bunkbeds and I had a top bunk. As a teenager, I would post pictures of Elvis Presley, Ricky Nelson and Fabian on the ceiling above my bed. When the addition to the house was built, we had a small room for an insider bathroom. However, it never got finished and we continued to have an outside outhouse until we moved to Michigan. In the early years, we also carried water up a slight hill from a natural flowing artesian spring from a creek below our home. The water was beautifully clear, cold and tasty. Eventually, we did get water from a well pumped into our home. We always had plenty to eat and my mom was one of the best Southern cooks. It seemed everyone, including us, had a garden and my uncle would kill a pig and share fresh meat with us. There were outings with our cousins to pick black berries, and a lot of Sunday dinners together. With our cousins, we would climb the pine trees across the road from our house. We lived fairly close to two of my mom's sisters and altogether there were a total of 13 kid cousins. There were family reunions in the summer with my mom's side of the family.

My Dad was musically talented. He played several string instruments; mainly the mandolin and electric guitar. Cousins, from my dad's side of the family, played piano, drums, guitar and bass guitar. Dad would invite musicians to play music at our home, or often we would go to someone else's home. Many times, dad would join musicians to form a band. The venues and occasions varied, such as weddings, birthdays and anniversaries held in homes, bars, skating rinks or other venues. Music was a positive in my life then and remains an enjoyment. I had fun with the people who came to our home and I enjoyed listening to the music and loved to dance. Mom offered good southern food. Living in North Carolina, these gatherings would often take place outside our home at bars. When we moved to Michigan, I didn't participate in these times at bars. I was mostly involved when we had people to our home on Friday and Saturday nights. Often, the music didn't stop until the early morning hours. It was hard to sleep until it ended. Always, there was alcohol and my dad would usually end up drunk. The night could end with him going to bed, or it could get loud and out of control. Even with the late nights and hard times, I claim memories of great country music and really good times.

Around 9 years of age, my dad was caught by federal agents making moonshine / white lightning in the mountains of North Carolina and was taken to jail. It was a federal offence; therefore, the trial was to be held at the federal courthouse in Richmond, Virginia. Mom took my brother Doug and I with her to the trial. I will never forget the austere and large courtroom. The judge, clothed in a black robe, sentenced my dad to 5 years in federal prison. Of course, we cried as they took Dad away. With good behavior, my dad served 3 years in Lewisburg, PA federal prison and was on probation when released. Dad would not identify to the authorities who he worked for. He was protecting the people and organization who hired him to help make and distribute illegal moonshine. For his silence, he was compensated by the organization providing some money to my mother for our family. My mom never talked about the details with us kids. The only way we know this is by what we observed. In Richmond, we therefore, stayed in a nice hotel. My mother could not afford a hotel. She worked hard to support us and would now be the total support for 3 children on her own. Another observation was one day we were in the hotel elevator going to our room. A man got into the elevator wearing a long overcoat. He handed my mom an envelope. I believe that envelope contained money, as Mom took it but never said to her nine- and five-year-old kids.

I was 12 years of age when dad returned home from prison. My happy days as an innocent kid ended. I don't remember the day the sexual abuse began, but I do know it was soon after he came home. My way of coping was to tense up and resist by not relaxing. I just wanted to get through it as quickly as possible. The details of the sexual abuse never included intercourse. Following each time, my dad would pucker up and ask me to kiss him just on the lips. The setup for me, the child, was the emotional blackmail. The setup was asking to do things, like go to a school event, spend overnight with a friend or cousins or other things I might want to do. He would always catch me alone or out of sight of Mom or other family members. Not every time but often If I asked or was asked to do things, I had to pay the price. The price was to allow him certain sexually abusive touching or actions involving my private parts. He told me, if I would tell Mom or anyone, no one would believe me or I would destroy the family. I was a child and I believed him. The emotional blackmail occurred sometimes when family or friends were present. I would ask or be invited to do something or go somewhere. Dad would find an obscure position out of the sight of others, so he wouldn't be seen. He would hold up three or more fingers. This gesture meant, if I said yes or was given permission to do it, I would have to pay the price.

Sexual abuse is not necessarily about sex. It can be about a person feeling powerless who obtains a feeling of power by control over a more vulnerable person. Abusing a young child, can provide opportunity to feel powerful. I am not a trained psychologist, but learning some of my dad's background he definitely had times when he was powerless. I understand that, still that does not change or excuse his abusive behavior. After I began working through my issues resulting from the abuse, I learned I felt dirty and bad, shameful. I blamed myself. In blaming myself, I thought "if only I didn't do things or want to go places it wouldn't have happened". There were times I didn't go places or do things, to avoid the abuse. Young children tend to blame themselves as they try, in their immaturity, to make sense of it all. I believe children love their parents, no matter what. I know I did and wanted their approval. An abused child takes responsibility onto themselves, and is confused in the relationship. I concluded; it must be me surely, I could have done something. I am bad, wrong.

While living in North Carolina before moving to Michigan, I was age fifteen and there was four of us kids. Mom had given birth to a second brother, about a year after dad came home from prison. I was about thirteen years old when he was born. We moved to Michigan in 1961. In Michigan, mom gave birth to a brother and sister. In total, I now had five siblings. Before my marriage in 1967, I lived with my baby brother until he was one year old. My baby sister was born about a year after my marriage. I loved them both and spent some time with them. However, I wasn't there for a large part of their childhood or in early teen years. First, when they were three and four years old; I had back surgery and blood clots developed in my lungs. This kept me down and unable to drive, as I was approximately 3 months in the hospital and it took about a year to fully recover. Secondly and later on, I missed time with them due to my confronting the sexual abuse.

I confronted my abuse as I healed three times. The first confrontation is when mom brought my middle sister to my apartment, I had been married two years. My sister had been running away or going out from the home, some of those times, mom had called me to go find her. However, she brought her over to my apartment this time. As I listened, my sister told mom what was happening to her and why she was getting out of the house. My dad had been abusing her. I had never told my mom about my abuse. When my sister told her story, I believed her right away. The pattern my dad used with my abuse was very similar to my sister's abusive experiences. I knew she was telling the truth. I told my mom the same things happened to me. I recognized dad's approaches and actions in her abuse. The second time I confronted was when my youngest sister was a teenager. I was on my healing journey, learning and healing. My moral compass was pulling on me to protect her. I think too, my sister role was confused with mothering my siblings. For sure I know, I had a strong desire to protect her. This time, I tried to talk to my sister directly to find out if she was being sexually abused by my dad. From my point of view, that did not go well. I confused and scared her and never for sure knew whether she was being abused. The third, and final, time I confronted occurred when I became aware a grandchild had been sexually abused. At this time, I had received a lot of help in counseling and done a lot of self-examination and healing. I knew, I was angry and my intention was to stop it. I asked all my siblings to meet with me and that I wanted to share something with them. They all agreed to meet me and mom was not asked to come, not sure if she knew? All came, except my middle sister was not there. As a result, when mom was told I found myself abandoned and not welcome to family events.

Mom worked outside the home all the years she was raising us kids. Dad worked outside the home, except for his 3 years in prison and he became disabled in Michigan. In North Carolina and while dad was in prison, mom would go to work early. My brother Doug and I would take my sister to a babysitter and then walk to the bus stop for school. In Michigan, dad wasn't employed long and had several back surgeries resulting eventually in him being disabled to work. Mom, and us kids, carried the load of responsibility. As the oldest sibling, I had way too much responsibility in caring for and watching out for my siblings. I also did paperwork in helping my mom pay family bills. I felt responsible to keep the peace and became involved at times in squabbles between siblings or mom and dad. I believe I was robbed of my childhood. This was a loss I had to learn how to grieve and let go. I was not a cherished child and nor was I nurtured to grow with love and direction.

I value children and life. It is my opinion, children are to be wrapped in the arms of loving parents who cherish, nurture and protect them. This allows kids to grow and develop into the person they were born to be. Kids are to be taught responsibility, which they learn as they grow up in a safety net of love and nurturing. With God's help, I have resolved this loss of childhood within myself. In caring for my brothers and sisters, I never blamed them for any of that loss. My role in the family was more one of mother than sister. Now, it brings me joy, knowing I have been given the gift of healthier and fun relationships with most of my siblings. I enjoy and have fun in building these relationships with siblings.

My parents had decided we should move to Michigan for the purpose of finding work. Dad had three brothers already living and working in Michigan. The family plan was for dad to come first, find work and find a place for us to live. He found work and made living arrangements and came back to North Carolina to move us. Plans were made to leave and I found it exciting, an adventure. We left NC and drove to Michigan in a panel truck. The things we took were clothes and personal items. Of course, we cried leaving our family and cousins. But we had no idea how different it would be. Emotionally, we had no clue the pain we would feel from leaving behind North Carolina sun, cousins, school and extended family. I was numb to feeling from the abuse, which was how I coped. I had developed, what I later on labeled, my Scarlett O'Hara Attitude. Scarlett O'Hara was a main character in the book and movie, "Gone with the Wind." When things were bad, Scarlett would say something like "I'll think about that tomorrow." This way of thinking would allow me to find a distraction, which was often fun and laughter or music.

It was not long living in Michigan and it became apparent, the adventure was not fun! Dad's original job had fallen through, not sure why. He ended up playing music in some of the bars around Grand Rapids. Most often he would drink too much and come home late hours. Mom and he often argued. Mom's solution was always to move back to North Carolina, which we never did. Due to this possible moving back solution, we didn't unpack boxes from North Carolina. Instead, they sat around the apartment for a while. Eventually, Dad and Mom secured jobs within the furniture industry. Mom had experience as a seamstress and dad as an upholsterer in the furniture industry. This was one of the reasons for coming to Grand Rapids for its' prominence in this industry. We lived in two different apartments on the west side of Grand Rapids. My oldest brother and I attended city schools, and lived in an ethnic Polish neighborhood. We were southerners speaking with our southern words. The kids at school had attended school together since kindergarten, so it was hard to relate and make friends. My brother was often in fights and I felt like I was in a prison. In less than two years, a house was purchased and we moved to Wyoming, Michigan. We now lived in a more suburb neighborhood and smaller school system. We were more content, but still missed North Carolina. I had attended the same North Carolina school for 8 ½ years, in Michigan I had moved three times, changed schools twice. I was 17 years old and still experiencing sexual inappropriate touching.

Circumstances began to happen my senior year of high school. I secured my driver's license, and began working as a cashier in a grocery store. I was driving, had my own car and was gone from the house more often. A couple times, dad was hospitalized for back surgery and had resulting periods of recovery. It was easier to protect myself. I could get away in my car, and avoid situations around the house. Dad's back surgeries and hospitalizations affected his mobility at times. Another change occurred early in my senior year; I met Charlie who became my boyfriend. Once I had a serious boyfriend, I felt even safer. Dad couldn't catch me off guard as easily. I learned how to manipulate and control my environment.

As I attended the Survivors for Incest group at the YWCA and processed memories and emerging feelings, understanding of self and resolution of issues came about. I accepted it was not my fault. I heard, what every survivor needs to hear, "it is not your fault."

While gaining clarification in the therapy group, I found myself having a lot of mixed emotions, bottled up confusion, fear and anger inside me. I found the courage to talk with Charlie about my fear of him and others harming Annie. Charlie gave me an example. He told me how much he loved his little sister, Susie. She was the youngest and he took care of her while his parents worked and his older brother and sister went to school. He recognized her being a young, playful little girl and his role was to protect her. In other words, he saw her innocence and his responsibility as older brother to protect and not harm her. The way he spoke, I knew this was Annie's Dad and he would never intentionally hurt her.

My mind was being renewed and my emotions healed. About one year in the YWCA program, the Y decided to change the program. Groups would be for 3-months, not unlimited or repetitive. Those who came to the program would be in a group for 3 months. If a participant felt they needed more help, the Y would provide referral information to other programs, a counselor, or a psychiatrist / psychologist. I was disappointed. It took a long time for me and others to begin trusting and opening up about the sexual abuse. Also, time was needed to sort out confusing thoughts and feelings. I had to decide "what next?" After being there for a year, I had gained a lot of understanding and healing. However, I still felt I had a lot of pieces to work out and needed more. I had a motivation and drive with me very strongly to understand what happened to me and change what I could. I wanted to be whole, live better. My decision was to begin counseling with a psychologist.

The psychologist I was referred to by a friend was a professor at Grand Valley University. He had been highly recommended by a counselor friend, I met in Al-Anon. Over a period of one year, we met two times a week, then once a week and slowly reducing visits to only as needed.

These one-to-one sessions with the psychologist helped me pull the pieces together. Together, we examined who I really was or wanted to be. We examined my thoughts, feelings and coping skills. I had a lot of pent-up anger from the abuse, and resentment or self-pity residing in me from the past. I would feel sorry for myself at times of disappointment, i.e., when things didn't go my way, when things would happen that I didn't understand or when I was unsure and emotionally upset. It is how I coped, poor me, poor me.... I would become confused. Confusion made me incapable of figuring things out or helping myself and it helped me avoid taking personal responsibility. It was easier when I could blame something or someone else, such as my poor childhood or Charlie's drinking. It was a vicious cycle; I would be disappointed and angry. Instead of taking responsibility and time to process circumstances or feelings, I would fall back into that "victim" mentality of "poor me." To take responsibility and face myself was scary. I was afraid of the feelings of abandonment, rejection, that I was not liked, or being labeled as a trouble maker, if I spoke up. My anger which was being masked by fear and justified by self-pity. It was a pattern of coping, I would feel sorry for myself, get confused, and justify poor me. The self-pitying little girl (Lynnie) would think "I am different, I don't know what to do, I can't help myself, no one else understands" and so the pattern of thinking would go. It was how I coped, easier to avoid or deny and I felt safer. However, it did not help me grow, live life abundantly or mature into the woman I was born to be. Self-pitying resentment kept me stuck in a cycle of disappointment and fear.

Arriving for a session with the psychologist, he would usually start by asking how I was feeling. Or, he might ask how was my day or what circumstance would I want to talk about. For a long time, when talking about the sexual abuse and exploring my feelings, I could not get angry with my dad. The anger came out against my mom, who did not protect me. I began to have nightmares. The psychologist advised me to get up and write everything I saw, was thinking or feeling from the night mare. He asked me then to bring my writing to our next session. One night I had a terrible nightmare, which I now truly believe God used that nightmare to open a door for me. The nightmare woke me up and I was shaking and scared. I got out of bed and began to write. The words flew onto the paper. I wrote really fast and a total of seven pages. I went back to bed and I took my writing to my next counseling session.

> *Note for consideration: An effective psychologist or counselor is one who is educated and licensed / certified by your state's licensing regulatory office. Your selection should be someone who is compassionate, remains professional not a close friend and is an active listener. A good counseling professional will not give you answers, they will give you examples, information, and feedback. They can help you explore setting boundaries in healing and learning healthy caring for yourself.*

As I shared the nightmare notes, I gained a lot of understanding. The nightmare was a scene of me standing over the kitchen sink washing dishes. Dad was standing next to me. (Dad would often come up behind me while I was at the kitchen sink washing dishes and no one was around and grab me inappropriately.) My Mom opened the kitchen door and looked in. Mom did not come in, but she closed the door and left me alone with my dad. Now, I understood why I was so angry with Mom for not protecting me. I was terrified of my dad and was still afraid to get mad at him.

My confidence was growing and I now had a support system consisting of professionals and friends. I was stronger and clearer about myself. I was being cared for and I had more ability to listen, to help and to love and help others unconditionally. I was strong enough now and when I made my final attempt to confront my family secret. As I said before, I asked all my brothers and sisters to meet with me. Of the siblings who came (4 of 5), there were different reactions. One brother believed me with no negative reaction, one believed and felt hurt / mad that I didn't tell him. This brother has a big heart, masked sometimes by his anger. He always thinks he can fix things. He was angry, as he thought he might have been able to help and he wondered about his own girls. The other siblings either didn't believe me or were in disbelief with nothing to say. I was so sad to share this with them about their dad. I knew telling them might result in consequences, and that I might not be believed. There was good potential of anger and rejection directed at me. However, I was convinced the secret had to be exposed and it was the right thing to do. To expose this secret in my family would give opportunity for stopping the abuse from happening to other generations. From the stories of others, education and from my own experiences, while I knew it would cause hurt and pain initially, the pattern of abuse had to be changed and the secret exposed. Following that meeting, I was estranged from my parents, brothers and one sister for a couple of years. I knew confronting the truth of the abuse was the risk to not be believed or apart of their lives anymore. No one physically called me or told me I was no longer a part of the family. I just would not be invited to any family gatherings, there just was no contact, no phone calls and no invitations from my parents and some of my siblings. Hindsight, I see there was a pattern in my family of not resolving conflicts. You were either in or out of the circle, depending on what you said or did. You could not go against the family belief of being "the perfect family" by telling the problems outside the family.

A couple years after that final confrontation, my mom was going to retire. She called me and invited me to her retirement party. Work was always important to my mom and she enjoyed the people she worked with. So, I did love her and I accepted her invitation to attend her retirement party. I knew this was a big deal in her life, and being a very prideful person, it took a lot for her to call and ask me. This is a gift of facing myself and healing my past. I understood my own humanity better and how imperfect humans are. I saw my mom as human and came to believe she loved as best she could. That doesn't excuse her adult behavior, as I too am accountable as an adult. But, understanding myself helped me to understand and forgive her. However, there were no verbal apologies or acknowledgements of the abuse and harm done to me. However, I was again invited to family gatherings like nothing had ever happened. The difference now, I knew myself and that I would protect my daughter and never leave her with her grandparents. I was strong enough to say no and leave situations, if I was uncomfortable. I trusted me more. I never left my daughter alone with my parents, nor did she ever spend the night with them.

The next step of healing for me, was confronting my dad directly. My parents were older, alone with no one else living in their home. Charlie and I were empty nesters, as our daughter, Annie, was living in Colorado. I had been regularly attending church, but one Sunday morning, I just knew it was time to confront my dad and my mom together. Instead of going to church, I drove over to my parents' home and my dad opened the door. I told dad I want to talk with him and Mom. Mom was at the kitchen table, where she was having coffee and a cigarette. I walked into the kitchen area, sat down and told them both I needed to talk with them. Of course, I was nervous. I was more confident, sure of myself, and no longer terrified of my dad.

Groundwork preparing me for this day of confronting dad, had been laid as I worked in my counseling sessions. It was suggested in one session, to write dad a letter telling him all I would say to him about the abuse and harm done to me. I did write a letter but never sent the letter. The letter did serve the purpose of helping me clarify my thoughts and feelings. Another time and within a counseling session, a therapist helped me confront dad, as if he was there. I was able to tell him what he did and how it affected me. I got angry with dad through that exercise and worked through those feelings toward him. The terror was gone.

In my parents' home and face-to-face with both parents, I began by saying how the results of the abuse made life more difficult. Emotions came and I was nervous, so this many years later I don't remember my exact words nor theirs. I tried to share specifically how being sexually abused had affected me and impacted my husband and daughter. Dad's reaction was silence, but he listened. I don't remember him saying a word. He did not deny it. Eventually he walked away my leaving me alone with Mom. Mom's reaction was one of questioning. Not remembering her exact words, I do remember the intent was to question me about how I handled the situation. She put the blame on me for not telling her when I was kid. Of course, she didn't like that I had told others. It seemed to me; she was saying I didn't handle it in the right way. Looking backwards, without doubt, I believe God led me to this confrontation. I did go with no expectation of what might result from telling them together. Mom's criticism of how I had shared my secret really didn't bother me. After all, I had told her directly once and twice second-hand through my siblings. I recall saying, something like, "well Mom there are not books about just how to go about this". Although nervous, I knew I had done nothing wrong and the abuse was my fault. I was stronger now in myself and no matter what they would say, I believed myself to have been a wonderful kid deserving of love, protection and to be treasured like all children. Mom did not ask any details and dad never came back into the room. My parents were adults and should have protected me. I knew going there I risked rejection and being blamed, which mom sort of did. It did not unsettle me. It was not easy and certainly awkward. There was no arguing or yelling, no bad words expressed to one another. It ended with mom saying she loved me and I left. No acknowledgement or apology.

Looking back, the day I confronted my parents together gave me more freedom. It allowed me to feel stronger and no more need of their approval or acknowledgement. I was an adult woman with

God-given power to make my own choices and not allow the behavior of others to control me due to my need for approval. I needed to face my dad especially, say it and survive emotionally. As I continued my healing journey from that point on, I was also able to reclaim good memories and positive things about my parents. For example, my dad was not an educated man but he would learn how to fix anything around the house. He was not afraid to try and learn from any house or mechanical repair experience. I gained that courage to paint in my home and tackle repairs without fear. I found figuring out those things a challenge. From my mom, as a commercial sewer, and I saw her love for sewing. I never sewed upholstery fabric, but I did learn how to use a sewing machine and easily made clothing repairs or sewed home projects, like curtains and gifts.

My growing relationship with God helped me forgive my parents. I came to understand forgiveness meant giving up the right to judge them. I was able to let go and leave the judgment to God. That was easier now after facing myself and seeing my own behavior in reality. Being human and imperfect, me and all of us are capable of doing wrong to others, committing wrong acts. One sin (wrong doing) is no greater than another. Only God can deliver pure justice. God is the all-merciful, infinite and loving judge who delivered me through his son Jesus Christ. I made the decision to believe in Jesus. When I am aware of my wrong doing, I know if I repent and turn from my wrong doing, I can ask for forgiveness. Then, I receive forgiveness and freedom. God's forgiveness through Christ never runs out.

Understanding my own behavior as a human being, this final confrontation with my parents and forgiving them, gave me more freedom in my living. I am sad that the relationships with my parents were more on the surface level and remained that way until my mom became sick with cancer. Mom was dying from cancer and in the hospital when she acknowledged the abuse. I was helping to bath her and she talked to me. She didn't label it childhood incest or sexual abuse, she called it "that awful thing between me and Dad." She simply said she didn't know what to do and she loved me. I recognize that as a gift not all abuse victims receive. Truly, a blessing from God. That simple statement told me she had thought about it and she believed me.

A year or more later and following Mom's death, dad became very ill with Hodgkin's Lymphoma and congestive heart failure. Dad had a period of time where he was going in and out of the hospital for various health issues. One of those times, he was very ill and had been in the hospital for a while. I believe he may have thought he was going to die? He was so sick. I visited him one evening with my brother Doug and his wife. The three of us were going out to eat after the visit. Dad asked me if I would stay a while and I said yes. When we were alone, dad brought up the abuse and apologized to me. He also acknowledged he had done the same thing to my sister. My sister was about 8 years younger than me. Like me, she was around 12-13 when the abuse began. Dad asked me to bring her to the hospital for him to talk with her. I asked her and she came with me and he talked to her. To have my abuser acknowledge his responsibility for what he did to me and my sister was a blessing, which sexual abuse survivors don't often receive.

The abuse was not my fault nor my sister's fault, we were both kids, pre-teens. When he took responsibility, it changed how I thought of him. Before, I thought he must be evil. As a kid, before I understood myself, it was easy to look at myself as evil because I loved him. Now, with more clarity and understanding, I looked at him as a sick, ignorant and elderly sick man in need of healing and help. When he went home from the hospital, I was there often and on Saturdays cleaning and taking care of him. It was easier for me to care for him now, just as I would have compassion for any other human being in his circumstance. Dad was a child of God, a human being who did wrong things and was ignorant about how to be a loving dad protecting his children. Some day he would stand before God and give an account of himself. God's grace helped me through my times together with dad before he died. I found a new sense of truth and honesty with him and was never afraid to tell him my truth or stand up for myself.

With both parents now deceased, looking back on this part of my story, I have no regrets. I was able to accept dad and mom, both the good and bad parts of their humanity, and acknowledge I loved them. My parents were responsible for their parenting and for what they did wrong. As adults, they are accountable to God. My sister and I are not to blame in any way for our abuse. As adults, my sister and I are responsible for our own behavior as adults.

These days, I hope and pray they both landed in heaven. We never had those conversations so I cannot know for sure what they believed. But I believe they were believers and don't question their faith. Mom, said she believed and she said to me one day "your dad believes in God more than you think." A friend of the family, told me dad had accepted Christ before he died. God's forgiveness through Christ can occur in a moment, such as the thief on the cross who asked Jesus to remember him when Jesus went into the kingdom. Jesus answered the thief "truly I tell you, today you will be with me in paradise." (NIV Luke 23:42-43)

CHAPTER VII

Why Open Up the Past?

N o one gets through this world without troubles and struggles of some kind. Trauma from abuse can be buried deep and every healing journey is individual to the person. There are similarities in our circumstances, thoughts, and feelings. We can support and learn from one another through our stories. Depending on your age, you may remember Elizabeth Smart? Elizabeth, a beautiful young girl age 14, kidnapped from her home at knife point during the night. She was taken from her own bed and held against her will for 8-9 months. Her kidnappers kept her camped out in the woods, and only about 18 miles away from her home. The kidnappers were husband-and-wife. The man raped her repeatedly. She was mentally and emotionally abused by both her abductors. She was eventually found and returned to her family. Elizabeth now shares publicly her story and her faith to inform and help others. Elizabeth says, "It is not what happens to us that defines us. It is how we choose to react that defines us."

Elizabeth Smart had a choice, following her horrendous circumstances, as to how she would move forward. Can you imagine what she and her family went through? As adults, we have choices how we will handle circumstances and past trauma in our lives. Circumstances of trauma, hurt, abuse etc. which causes confusion, destroys trust and innocence, and causes pain. We decide are we going to let the pain define us for a lifetime and hold us back from life? Are we going to live like victims or as survivors, overcomers? Do we take back our individual power by opening up to the pain and healing? Do we walk through the pain exposing our losses, hurts, anger and rage? Are we willing to work and learn how to deal with our feelings? Can we begin to see and understand our pain-filled memories? Will we risk seeing ourselves honestly and change negative behaviors? Do we expose harmful secrets we have kept hidden that lock us up inside? The bottom line, it is up to each of us to decide how to answer these questions and decide what choices we will make. We can live as victorious survivors, not as victims. Other people can add to my happiness. However, my personal happiness and wholeness in living doesn't depend on anyone but me. The responsibility for my life is between me and God. Like Elizabeth, I no longer allow my past to define me. I continue to learn from my past, but I do not live in the past.

By exposing the secret, acknowledging and walking through the pain helped me to begin healing. I embarked on a healing journey, which has helped me develop healthier relationships with myself, God and others. Emotionally and mentally wounded people who remain victims, will hurt and wound others. If we don't seek understanding by learning and renewing our minds, facing ourselves honestly and seek help to resolve our pain, then we pass along generational family dysfunction. In my own life and through stories others have shared, I have seen that wounded people with victim mentality will intentionally and unintentionally hurt others. We especially can hurt those closest to us; i.e., spouses, children, extended family and friends. As an example, I treated Charlie harshly at times. A specific incidence, before I began healing from my abuse, comes to mind. Charlie came up behind me in the kitchen while I was washing dishes. He wrapped his arms around me touching my breasts. I was immediately startled and so angry. I yelled at him, and pushed him away. The circumstance left me frustrated. I felt bad about myself and did not know why I was so angry. I knew he was my husband

and I could have responded as a loving spouse being pleasantly surprised. I could have turned around to hug him back. When I began working through the pain of my sexual abuse, looking back at that incident I realized, I was reacting out of my past. Dad would come up from behind, in the kitchen, if we were alone. He would put his hands on my breasts or pinch me on the buttocks. Charlie was my husband and he was being intimate and loving, he was not my dad. The anger was coming from my suppressed anger I had never acknowledged with my dad. With dad I felt unsafe and fearful and could not get angry with him. The overreaction of anger was due to the past experiences with my dad, it had nothing to do with Charlie. Charlie was tender and I felt safe with him. My reaction had nothing to do with Charlie, but had everything to do with my unresolved feelings toward my dad's actions.

Why look at the past or get help for past trauma and emotional pain? The answer I come to is, so we learn how to live fully! Living life to the fullest encompasses dealing with what comes into our days and lives. Sometimes it is joy, sadness, excitement and other feelings. Looking at our true and honest reaction to what happens each day. We can learn not to make choices out of negative, angry or fearful feelings but to take the time needed to process. By allowing ourselves time, we can decide upon the choice to make or the action to take. Sometimes we come to the conclusion to do nothing. We learn to "let go and let God."

If you or members of your family (kids) are currently fearful or unsafe, get yourself and or them immediately to a place of safety. You can then sort things out and be safe while doing so. Many communities have safe houses and public health departments along with police, pastors and other help organizations to help you.

There are traumatic and physical causes to mental illness. Please consider a mental illness is to be diagnosed and treated by a psychiatrist. If you think you have a mental illness, go to a licensed credentialed psychiatrist for evaluation. Treatment may include medication to be prescribed by the psychiatrist. If you have been told or you suspicion you may have a mental illness, please do not take that first step of consciousness into your past trauma, nor act on your thoughts of hurting yourself or others. You are important and please seek help. Your doctor or community mental health organization can help you. For a period of time, you may need inpatient care. Talk to someone, get with someone for support and ask them to go with you for help. Perhaps your support is that of a close family member, a friend, counseling professional or your pastor. There is no shame in asking for help and you are a human person of value and deserving of all life has to offer. How do I know? Because, I have experienced feeling shameful, worthless, confused and alone. DO NOT give up on you! The shame and worthlessness you might be feeling is not real, you have come to the wrong conclusion about yourself, just as I did. You can find someone to help, such as a school counselor teacher, pastor, friend, or trusted family member. If you approach a church or pastor for help, don't give up if the reception is not helpful. Go to another church. God is with us in every effort we make. YOU are unique and valuable, DO NOT let anyone, tell you otherwise.

CHAPTER VIII

Learning to Walk with God and Not Alone

Where does my help come from when I am on my own? No longer a victim, when I face emotional, hurtful, and confusing circumstances and my support network is not immediately available, where do I go? God is always available at any time and in all places.

When I hit my bottom and began Al-Anon, I did not know God nor did I see any evidence of his presence in my life. Off and on, I went to church. I knew some of the right spiritual or religious sayings like, "God is always good", "God can't give you more than you can handle" and "saved by the blood of Jesus." The truth is I was ignorant of my true spiritual condition. I had no clue of what it meant to have a relationship with God. My thinking was going to church on Sunday, and doing the right things. I operated on a faith still based on what I did or failed to do. There was a list in my head of what I thought was "the right things to do as a Christian". It really all depended on me. When someone says "I don't go to church because people there are hypocrites" now I can smile and think this is exactly why I go. None of us are perfect, we are all capable of being hypocrites. I need renewal each week and repetition in hearing God's word from the Bible.

Early on in attending church, I was so afraid of sounding ignorant and saying the wrong thing I wouldn't ask questions. My involvement in church was learning what was expected and doing or saying that. In other words, being a Christian was based on what I did. It was dependent on me to do the right thing. God would fix it, if I could only figure out the right thing to do or say in all circumstances; God would make my life wonderful, "wouldn't he?"

We talked in Al-Anon about a higher power. Al-Anon's Twelve Traditions were a guiding structure for guiding group actions and meetings. The Twelve Steps and Traditions of AA and Al-Anon support not discussing specific religions, politics or any controversial views in meetings. God, is the universal name of a higher power and is mentioned in literature. No specific religious tenant or the names of Jesus and Holy Spirit is to be discussed in meetings. In telling personal stories, individuals could share what they believed. The reason for avoiding controversies and religion is to prevent diversion from the principles we were learning and practicing to help ourselves. On a person-to-person basis, outside of meetings, we would talk about faith in God and Jesus Christ. When I began Al-Anon, my attitude was one of anger toward God. Of course, I wouldn't share that because you don't get angry with God, that is not right. I thought "God? Hum…I sure can't see where he has done anything at all for me!" I learned it was important to keep the focus on myself, as I listened to others and worked through the 12-Steps. It would not have been helpful to me, if meetings evolved into discussions of religious books, political views, theology or religion. My view of God was mostly agnostic. I was angry at God for not doing anything for me, so I thought. When I would hear someone, outside of meetings talk about Jesus, I was a little softer on Jesus. I related to the Jesus I had seen in old photographs or paintings. The famous painting of the Last Supper is how I saw Jesus. Jesus' face always looked peaceful and kind.

A woman, Nita I knew from Al-Anon, befriended me and was a follower of Jesus Christ. Nita and I talked on the phone often in early Al-Anon years. We would talk about God, Jesus and the Bible. One day on the phone, she brought up the devil and remembering that call, I laugh at myself. I said to her, "I am just learning about God, I don't even want to know about the devil." Another memory, I was attending an Al-Anon meeting. Irene, a very kind and sweet woman, was our Al-Anon group representative and handled our literature sales. At the time, I was just beginning Al-Anon. I approached Irene to buy an Al-Anon book and I asked her, "will Al-Anon go against my religion?" Again, I laugh at myself. I had no understanding of faith or relationship with God, nor the differences in religions. This kind woman smiled, patted my hand and responded "I think in time you will find they (Al-Anon and religion) will go hand-in-hand." She didn't judge me; she didn't try to convert me. She taught me through her kindness and gentleness. Eventually, as I got to know her, I observed and learned from her devotion to God. She became to me a living example of life lived, faith in something greater than herself (God) and she was accepting and non-judgmental of others.

My personal relationship with God, and what that meant, began when I started Al-Anon. Identifying my religious affiliation took time. My first engagement with religion began when I was sixteen. I had the desire to go to church and began seeking a church. Since I was a southerner, I selected a Southern Baptist Church. I was baptized by being immersed fully into the water. It seems I may have selected the Baptist religion because, in North Carolina, most the people around me were Southern Baptist. For about one to two years. I attended that church and got involved. I began to think I could never be there or get involved enough to be right, be acceptable. Of course, I didn't share my thoughts with anyone at the church. I kept my thoughts to myself and went through the motions; twice on Sunday and once on Wednesday for prayer meeting. I started to find excuses not to go. The church's evangelism committee visited people who were falling away from the church. Eventually they began visiting me on evangelism night. I would hide when they came to my house or, when I started driving and had a car, I would be gone. Avoidance was how I handled that circumstance. Of course, I felt bad. By not dealing openly and honestly with myself, I added more baggage to my bundle of hidden shameful and worthless feelings. I never went back to the Baptist church nor any church until after marriage.

Eight years or so later and after marriage and before I began Al-Anon, things were getting more difficult as the drinking increased. Again, I began seeking a church. This time I selected a Lutheran church. I made that choice based on my mom telling me my grandmother, her mom, had been Lutheran. I got involved in the Lutheran church by teaching a kindergarten Sunday school class. This was my attempt to do the "right thing." "Surely, if I do the right thing and went to church, God would fix my life", so I thought. Going to church did not fix things. This attempt to fix it was not working. My life was not getting fixed.

The church, organized religion, was not my first source of help. I continued to attend the Lutheran church occasionally, and certainly on holidays. After I began attending Al-Anon meetings, I became more honest and open to learning about religion and God. My connection with God and growing spiritually began with the Serenity prayer, which we would say at the beginning of all AA and Al-Anon meetings.

> *"God grant me the Serenity to accept the things I cannot change, the courage to change the things I can and the wisdom to know the difference."*

That prayer is so powerful. It brought me squarely into relationship with God. I was asking God for peace and to accept things beyond my control. Also, I was asking him to give me wisdom and courage to change things affecting me that I could control. This prayer helped me feel stronger within myself and peaceful. I had an ever-present partner; it wasn't all up to me. I didn't feel so alone. In the daily circumstances of life, instead of bottling things up inside myself, I would talk about them more readily. I would ask Al-Anon friends and mentors questions. I became a "people watcher", especially at church and in Al-Anon. I was learning to identify acceptable and unacceptable behavior. I learned what things in my life I was responsible for and I could never control any person other than myself. This peace, courage and wisdom came from God. Now, I could "Let Go and Let God!"

When my daughter, Annie, was born and I had been about 8 years in Al-Anon, instead of sporadic attendance, I began regularly attending the same Lutheran church. Having this baby girl motivated that drive in me to be the best person and mom possible. I wanted Annie to start out in the church, and to be baptized as an infant. Baptizing her as an infant was important to me, as I felt she would be under God's protection. Charlie was supportive of the baptism. Charlie being Latvian, it was customary to name a Godmother and Godfather. Both Charlie and I wanted Annie to have all the "right things" so she wouldn't feel outside of others in church and extended family. We had the same pastor who helped direct Charlie to AA officiate at her baptism at Zion Lutheran Church. After church service, we celebrated with family and friends in our home. I would take her to church on Sundays, and carry her up to the communion rail, while I took communion. Annie would receive a blessing. The pastor would make the sign of the cross in anointing oil over her forehead. I felt peaceful at the alter and felt that I was doing something good for Annie; placing her under God's protection.

Due to healing in Al-Anon and at the YWCA group therapy sessions, I was seeing things from a less fearful and more honest prospective in terms of my abuse, how I had coped with it and how the abuse impacted my life. I don't remember how old Annie was, I know she was a toddler when I decided to quit going to church. I stopped going to church for two primary reasons. First, I had more than I could handle with caring for home, a young daughter, attending Al-Anon, working part-time and YWCA group therapy. Secondly, I looked at that innocent precious daughter and knew I was still such a phony hypocrite. I still did not know or understand God. At my core, I was not sure I believed in God, how to follow

Jesus or should be going to church. My thought was "If I don't believe in God or understand the importance of church, what am I reflecting to Annie? If I continued this way of pretense, then what am I teaching my daughter?"

Annie was age 5 or 6, when I decided to go back to church. I went back to the Lutheran church. I had more understanding and knowledge about God and church. With gratitude, I was acknowledging God's presence and help in my life. No longer angry at God, I had begun seeing God as a Loving Father and seeing his presence in the details. God was in the process of healing my heart. I had a desire to learn more about God, religion and the purpose of attending to church. So, it was logical to begin church again. Still, I felt unworthy 'and could not take communion without crying.

As I attended church and continued Al-Anon, I began to see God's grace and presence more dramatically in my life. I had two events occur, which brought me deeper in my faith. These events brought to me a clear awareness of God's grace in my healing. Al-Anon called such events "spiritual awakenings".

The first event occurred shortly after my YWCA group therapy ended. In a session with the psychologist, I arrived and he asked "how are you?" I responded with a self-pitying tone, and a poor-me attitude, "I don't know where to begin." The psychologist said to me, "Linda life is like a circle just jump in." Feeling quite sorry for myself I began. I said "nobody in my life has ever truly loved me." Immediately, inside my head, a very clear and loud thought arose "but my grandma."

I only knew one of my grandparents. It was my grandmother on my dad's side of the family. She died when I was between twelve and thirteen years old. My parents, with me, had lived with my dad's parents for about a year. I was a toddler and my grandpa died while I was still very young. I didn't really know him or have memories of him. Grandma, at some point, moved closer to her daughter, and that was also closer to us. I began spending more time and overnights with her. Together, she and I would spend time on the back porch of her home, where she taught me how to crochet. The downstairs apartment she lived in was part of a very large house divided into several apartments. The house had wood siding, which had weathered and blackened on the outside. There was a full porch across the front and back of the house. Grandma was a small, thin woman with very long brown hair which she would pin up into a bun at the back of her head. As a Pentecostal, she didn't believe in cutting her hair. She would pray with me and take me to the Pentecostal church, which was a small church and preaching would go on for a long time. I witnessed people speaking in tongues and that did not frighten me. I did not understand what it meant, but I was not afraid of it. People were kind and would allow anyone to sing for the glory of God. My cousin Cindy and I would go up front and sing old hymns. Cindy and I were not singers. However, this small country church accepted us and what we offered. The length of time and the speaking in tongues did not put me off, I don't remember complaining to Grandma? A wonderful memory I have is a time when I spent the night with Grandma. I had an earache. Grandma put warm olive oil in my ear, and placed a cotton ball on the inside to keep the warm oil in and air out. She gently laid her hands on me, and prayed for my ear to heal. The whole experience still feels loving as I recall it.

The psychologist helped me that day to grieve the loss of my grandma. In that process of acknowledgment and tears, I gained back all those things Grandma did, which were gifts of love and caring. This day, I know she loved me and she loved God. Not only did I process the loss of my grandma, which had been buried for years, but I gained so much in understanding of love. I could no longer say nobody loved me. As I look back over the years and my struggles, I remember that many times the thought would come "God is the answer." I just didn't know how to get the answer. I believe this thought was a priceless gift. The thought sprung from seeds my grandma planted within me. She loved me, took me to church, and prayed over me and for others. She taught me about God's love through her words and prayers.

The second event occurred on a Saturday morning in my home. My daughter, baby Annie, was a really good sleeper. Annie was asleep, and I was sitting in the kitchen. Charlie was working overtime, so he was not at home. I began to read from the Al-Anon daily meditation book, "One Day at A Time in Al-Anon." A thought entered my mind, and I so clearly heard "you know Linda you have done some things that are pretty good" and the thoughts continued "you have done some things not so good, but it doesn't matter what you do, I love you." Those thoughts brought me to tears. I not only was loved by Charlie, friends in Al-Anon and my grandma but now I felt loved by God and understood the gospel of Christ. I could never have fixed myself, by working to always do the right thing. I did need to get honest with myself and I was taking responsibility for all aspects of my life. However, my worth was never about doing "the right thing to feel worthy or to be loveable". The answer was relationship with God. God had already done for me, through the cross and resurrection of Jesus Christ, that which I could never do for myself. I could not be perfect and do everything right; I would never have all the knowledge and answers for all of life's struggles; I could never do enough to earn God's love and I could not fix myself. God loved me so much he sent his son, Jesus, to suffer and die for my wrongs. The good news, Jesus rose again. My forgiveness is assured, when I turn away from my wrongs and ask God for forgiveness. There is nothing I can do to separate me from the love of God. God's love was not conditional. God's love is unconditional and he loves me. God was and continues to heal my emotions and provides me with wisdom in my choices through prayer and his word in the Bible. The gospel, good news, is not just for me, but for everyone on earth. Freedom comes from belief and faith in Christ. God's love and forgiveness is free and available to each person. Since that day, my self-worth began growing stronger and faith grew. I no longer cried at the church communion rail. I was now convicted by that experience, no one on this earth can take away my self-worth or identity as a child of God.

For the rest of my life on earth, I will never be alone. God is everywhere, available all the time, and I can talk to God any time through prayer. God created me with an identity and unique purpose, which only I can fulfill. I believe this is true for everyone. Each person is of value and has a unique purpose. God is creator and restorer of life. God confirms this to me all the time, not only in the details of my life, but in the lives of others around me.

As I continue to grow in my relationship with God, I recognize I do get lonely for human companionship. I can be lonely for human involvement, but I never feel alone. God's presence shows up in different ways, sometimes dramatic and other times subtly. God's presence has been apparent in unexpected and simple ways in my life. A few examples:

- a phone call from a friend when I most need it
- an unexpected conversation with a stranger while shopping or waiting in a doctor's office
- working outside in my flower garden and a neighbor stops by
- a special unexpected gift, perhaps money, that comes and meets a desire or need
- a church sermon, a video series, books, music, listening to other people of God, religious conferences and retreats, and, most of all, from the Bible, God's Word.
- I see God's creation and presence in the beauty of his creation; such as the variety of trees, flowers, grasses, animals and the changing of seasons
- beautiful music that encourages me of all genres; I learn from Christian music that contains God's inspired words from scripture

There are many ways I am aware of God in each day and all that I do. Daily I have so many opportunities to see God's presence, which I like to say "seeing God's face." Sometimes while listening to a song, a TV program, seeing a movie, or reading a book; a thought comes into my mind and enlightens me. The thoughts, bring me direction and clarity, which can help me in many ways. It may help me understand a current circumstance, bring clarity and direction about a decision or understanding in a relationship. God's presence is there in our lives, all around us if we listen and open our eyes.

Importance I Found in Reading the Word: I have, in most recent years, been more committed to reading the Bible regularly. When I read the Bible, there are times when I don't understand. Often, I will look up words and verses on a bible website, http://www.biblegateway.com. At times, I will consult the dictionary or a concordance to help me understand. My Bible has an introduction to each chapter, which helps me know the author, history of the times and key points of the book of the Bible. I pray before reading words such as "God open my ears to hear, heart to understand and mind to renewal through your word." I don't always understand God's Words or how God is directing me. Other times, the words will jump out at me and I think "WOW, why did I not know this before?" I struggled with reading the Bible and had thoughts like "where do I start reading, in the Old or New Testament?" Often, I would get started in a certain direction, then not be consistent or get bored, and give up. There are tons of daily reading plans available in various forms. You can find reading plans in many ways and explore varied versions of the Bible, which often have reading plans within them. I would read or hear that I should start reading in a certain book of the Bible, or so many chapters a day. Whatever plan I was looking at, I would begin, get overwhelmed and give up.

God's direction came to me through a Sunday morning sermon at church. The pastor suggested we begin reading the Bible starting with the New Testament. He said relax and read it as a novel, a love story. This direction came to me the summer following my husband's death. I decided to try it and made a commitment to read the entire New Testament over the summer. It worked for me, I got hooked. All summer, I learned so much and became much stronger in my relationship with God. My faith and understanding of God's character and his will grew. This experience convicted me of the necessity for reading God's Word. I learned reading God's word, was essential to my spiritual growth and helped me learn how to live as a Christian. At times, I would be reading and get so excited. The excitement would bring tears of joy to my eyes.

There are those who say the Bible is no longer relevant, out of date, and the world is different now so it doesn't mean the same. I do not believe that prospective at all. Even, if someone can't read, there are audio books and the bible is available online to listen to it. It will change a life, as it continues to do so in mine.

The people of the Bible are as real and human, back then, as we are in this day and time. I struggled with denial, insecurity and, many times, had no clue what to do in relationships. For example, David was a young shepherd boy who killed Goliath and eventually became King of Israel. David was in the generational line of Jesus. David was a human capable of good and evil. David became King. To simplify, I related to his humanity. David lusted after Bathsheba and she got pregnant. Bathsheba could not deny the King according to the laws of the time. Her husband, Uriah, was off fighting a war for King David. David didn't take responsibility for his actions instead he tried to cover up his wrong doing. David had Bathsheba's husband, Uriah, come home from the battlefield to sleep with his wife. David hoped it would appear Uriah was the father. Uriah was a loyal, honorable man and would not sleep with his wife. Due to Uriah's code of honor, his fellow warriors were still on the battlefield and could not have such pleasure. So, Uriah denied himself of the pleasure of sleeping with Bathsheba. King David had a dilemma, what to do? King David still doesn't take responsibility. He comes up with another plan to cover up his wrong doing. David sends his messenger to the battlefield, with a message to Uriah's commander. David's message said to put Uriah on the front lines of battle. David knew Uriah would be killed. This was David's solution to his problem. David solved his problem at the expense of Uriah's life. Once Uriah was gone David could take Bathsheba for his wife. Uriah returned to the battlefield and was killed. King David added murder to adultery. King David marries the widow, pregnant Bathsheba. Their child did not live.

Eventually, David was confronted by God's prophet, Nathan. Nathan used storytelling to confront David about his adultery and murder. David's heart was broken, he confessed and turned back to God. David was human in need of redemption. David did not learn from that, as a human he was still capable of wrong doing. His next wrong doing was to his daughter, Tamar. Tamar was raped by her half-brother, Amnon. When David found out, he was angry. Still, he did not address his son's bad behavior honestly. David maintained the family secret. This denial of harm done to Tamar, is similar to the family who continues to hide family secrets. The story of Tamar is much like stories of sexual abuse and family secrets, dysfunction in today's world. Tamar was scorned and not supported by love and truth, acknowledgment that she did nothing wrong. David's failure to deal with it openly, honestly within their family only led to anger and more problems within the family. For more details of the story, read 1 Samuel and 2 Samuel books of the Bible.

David's family history included adultery, murder, deceit, family abuse and dysfunction (generational sin.) David enabled his children in wrong behavior. Looking at the people of the Bible and seeing their humanity, convicts me the Bible is most relevant in today's world. There are examples of how to live and what behavior builds life and what behavior tears life down. The Bible is the greatest psychology book in the world and it was inspired by an infinite all-loving God. The Bible declares everyone valuable and deserving of love, as well as hold each person accountable for their own choices. I can identify with the people in these stories of the Bible. I find answers and hope.

The two largest obstacles to my spiritual growth, are my unwillingness to make time for reading, study, prayer and gathering with other Christians. Daily devotions and prayers are a priority. At times, I slip in my efforts....and then I re-commit to the most important relationship of my life and get back to it.

> *"When helping others, are you being selfish or self-caring? Selfishness; is seeking your own personal profit or pleasure. Self-caring is looking after your personal health, emotional and mental well-being. Sacrificing our fleshly pleasures is sometimes necessary to help and love others. Equally important, is being able to say "no", in order to take care of yourself. We are responsible to care for ourselves so we can care for others."*

<u>Importance of Prayer in My Life:</u> Prayer is conversation with God and being quiet to listen. I especially like sitting on my porch and looking out on nature, when I study and pray. God is omnipotent and knows my heart. God knows how I am feeling, as he created me and gave me feelings. Feelings help me understand what is going on inside of me, what I need to pay attention to. So, it is impossible to hide from God. I can talk to him, yell out my anger at Him, he already knows what's up. He knows my thoughts. He knows the trouble within me. If I harbor anger and unforgiveness, He knows. Praying it out to him, God will help me. Be yourself with the all loving, merciful and all-knowing creator God.

My husband and I were friends with a Catholic Nun who attended AA. One day I was talking with her and said "when I get down on my knees to pray everything goes through my mind, I can't focus, and it feels like I am there for hours but it was only a minute. However, when I am standing at the sink washing dishes, working with my hands, or out in nature digging in the flower garden, my mind is free. It is then that clear prayer flows from within." She told me it didn't matter how I prayed but that I prayed. She said perhaps

God has given you a prayer life of activity. Her prospective helped me relax. I didn't put the expectations on myself of praying in a specific "right" way, nor to pray in a certain holy position. The physical position in praying could be sitting, standing, walking or otherwise and was not of great importance. It was most important that I pray, and that I approach God the Father with the attitude of reverence, thanksgiving, respect and humility. My holy prayerful position was my attitude in praying not physical position. I can pray at any time, any place and in any physical position.

While writing this book, I had multiple health issues arise, and I was not sleeping well and dealing with chronic pain. I became overwhelmed and anxious. The anxiety could only be squelched by my acknowledgement that I was not in control. I had done all I could physically, such as keeping doctor appointments, exercising as I could and taking prescribed medication. Emotionally, mentally and spiritually, I needed to pray and take it to God. God is faithful and, once again, God provided peace. The following scripture helped me let go, let God.

> Philippians 4:6 – 7 (NIV) *"(6) Do not be anxious about anything, but in every situation, by prayer and petition, with thanksgiving present your requests to God. (7) And the peace of God, which transcends all understanding will guard your hearts and your minds in Christ Jesus."*

There are prayers and Psalms I say, when I am in a dry period or stressful time, lacking for words and having a hard time focusing. Here are some prayers or Psalms which bring me connection with the peace only God gives.

SERENITY PRAYER

God grant me the Serenity to accept the things I cannot change, the courage to change the things I can and the wisdom to know the difference.

The Serenity Prayer tells me God will give me peace to accept all things that are beyond my control. God will show me, if there are things I can change or do to help myself or others. God will teach me the difference. I will become aware of when to be quiet, step back from someone or situation to get a new prospective, when I am enabling and not helping and when I need to "Let Go and Let God."

LORD'S PRAYER

Our Father who art in heaven, hallowed by that name. Thy kingdom come; thy will be done on earth as it is in heaven. Give us this day our daily bread and forgive us our trespasses as we forgive those who trespass against us. Lead us not into temptation but deliver us from evil. For thine is the kingdom and the glory, forever and ever. Amen.

The Lord's Prayer was taught by Jesus to his disciples, when they asked Jesus "how should we pray." I am reminded in this prayer God is to be reverenced, God will provide for me, and God will deliver me. God forgives me and I am to forgive others. All honor and glory to God forever.

PSALM 23:1 – 6
A Psalm of David

The Lord is my Shepherd; I lack nothing. He makes me to lie down in green pastures. He leads me beside quiet waters. He refreshes my soul. He guides me along the right paths for his name's sake. Even though I walk through the darkest valley, I will fear no evil, for you are with me; your rod and your staff they comfort me. You prepare a table before me in the presence of my enemies; you anoint my head with oil, my cup overflows. Surely your goodness and love will follow me all the days of my life and I will dwell in the house of the Lord forever.

In the 23rd Psalm, I learn God is my Shepherd, my leader. God does and will comfort me, and guide me into right living. God restores me mentally and emotionally. He gives me peace in my mind and understanding. God heals my wounded heart. It is up to me, to trust him and not allow fear to rule my life.

CHAPTER IX

Choices.... Not a Victim but a Survivor

It is my belief that God created me and humanity with free will and freedom to make choices and God will not make someone follow Him. God allows life to unfold in a way we experience the consequence of our choices and actions. I have made my choice to believe in God, and to submit my will to His will, His way. Further, I accept His son, Jesus Christ, as my Savior and to follow Christ's example as it is taught in the Bible. I aspire to grow closer to Christ growing as a true Christian, a Christ Follower.

I think God gets a bad rap. It seems when bad things happen, God is an easy target. If only God would change it. If he is God, He could make it better. In reality, sometimes bad results are due to our own bad choice or wrong action. You may have heard, "if God is so loving, why would He allow an unfavorable or tragic event to happen? I understand people in pain need to make sense of it, often by blaming God or another person. I was angry with God, and I believed he could change my circumstances.

When I began my healing journey, I never connected my unhappiness and behavior with my free will or my choices. I felt sorry for myself and blamed others. I thought, no one understands me. In truth, as a child, I was a victim. However, as an adult, I continued to add to the resentment, blaming and not learning about choices I could make to help myself. This continued coping strategy just added to my unhappiness. I sank deeper into a victim mentality feeling sorry for myself. The list of things to feel sorry for me were multiple, such as:

- back surgery and blood clot in my lungs at 23 years old (not expected, out of work for year, lack of income would delay buying a house and having a child) .... disappointment, self-pity
- 4-5 years into my marriage was told I would never have children.... disappointment, self-pity
- stress on Charlie had increased, marriage became more troublesome and drinking increased.... disappointment, self-pity
- drinking increased and environment in our home filling with anger....... disappointment, self-pity
- increased drinking, deterioration of marriage, holidays ruined, no children......disappointment, self-pity

The list of disappointments grew and self-pity increased. I had adopted a victim mentality. It allowed me to feel sorry for myself. I could always find something or someone to blame for my behavior. A deep reservoir of self-pity existed in me. There was no one else who would understand, I am different. I was self-absorbed in my pain and didn't see I had any responsibility for my misery. I would look to outside forces, others to blame. It could always be God's fault, as he was responsible for everything. If God is so good and powerful, why didn't He change it? Poor, poor me.

Learning how to take care of myself emotionally and understanding came gradually. My attitude and behavior changed. When disappointment and things I didn't like happened, I began to look within for understanding. I need to examine my thinking and feelings. Tools were available to help me in a variety of ways. The Al-Anon slogan "Let Go and Let God" became a simple reminder for me. The slogan allowed me, in circumstances beyond my control, to turn things over to God for help and direction. I have seen evidence in my life and the lives of others where good came out of bad circumstances. A scripture verse, I believe with all my heart and which establishes this truth, is Romans 8:28 (ESV):

> *"And we know that in <u>ALL things</u> God works for the good of those who love him, who have been called according to his purpose."*

Don't blame others, there is no life in the blame game, there is only a well of self-pity, judgement and blame which grows deeper as you play the game. Sometimes we make the wrong choices, but God can even take mistakes and turn them around resulting in good.

CHAPTER X

Spiritual Growth in Helping Others

For 7-10 years in Al-Anon, as mentioned previously, Charlie and I were involved in AA and Al-Anon service work. Step #12 of the "Twelve Steps of Al-Anon and AA", is called the service step:

> *"Having had a spiritual awakening as a result of these steps, we tried to carry this message to others and to practice these principles in all our affairs."*

This twelfth step calls us, through gratitude for our own healing, to share and help someone else. We help by carrying our message of experience, strength and hope to others. Serving others helped Charlie and I to grow spiritually and emotionally.

For ten years, I was helping in some capacity the Healing Hearts / Journey Group ministries. Through both Al-Anon and Healing Hearts, I witnessed God's redeeming work in the lives of people. Observing people live more productive and happier lives, was a privilege and humbling. The next part of the healing was to see them then reach out to help others. I saw God's power in redeeming and healing lives. I will always remain open to sharing with anyone God puts in my path. Hearing people tell the story of their lives and being able to see God's redemption in those lives; I felt like I was standing on "holy ground." I truly believe we can get help from a lot of sources. In reading my story, you know I did get a lot of help.

However, I truly believe it is God that heals those pent-up, packed-down emotions of the heart. God looks upon our hearts and knows them. In Psalm 34-18 (NIV) states "The Lord (God) is close to the brokenhearted and saves those who are crushed in spirit."

Attending a non-denominational church, is where I became involved in Healing Hearts Journey Groups. Reading a Sunday service bulletin, I saw a new group was beginning out of the church's Care Ministries, Healing Hearts for survivors of sexual abuse. It pulled at me to go. I was drawn to find out about this ministry. I only knew at the time a desire to deepen my understand and relationship with God and other people. The group consisted of a leader, co-leader and 6 to 8 people, maximum size set for an effective group. We used a curriculum, which had been prepared by Open Hearts Ministry out of Kalamazoo, MI. Open Hearts Ministry was started by Sandy Burdick. Sandy had a need for her own healing and began a healing heart group in her church. Through Sandy, and others participating in the group, a lot of prayers were offered on next steps. Sandy collaborated with Dan Allender, a Christian Psychologist and author of "The Wounded Heart" to write and develop a 12-week biblically-based curriculum for those affected by sexual abuse.

When attending the group, as a participant, each week my leaders would begin by sharing their understanding of the topic. In the first sessions of group, a leader would share their own story. Participants were asked to read and work through some questions related to each week's topic to prepare for group. After the leaders shared their stories, the leaders would invite each participant to share their personal story. A lot of trust is necessary to share a personal story of woundedness, one feels vulnerable afterwards. Some do not feel safe enough to share and their choice is respected. For me, at this point I had already had a lot of healing and shared my story multiple times. To be in a group and within God's house, the church, talking about sexual abuse was so freeing for me. After my participation in the second 12-week group, I wanted to help others be free. I decided to attend the week-long training so I could be a group leader. I had such a passion and desire to help others feel the freedom I felt. I wanted them to also know God cared about healing their past and giving them a hope and a future.

> Jeremiah 29:11 *"For I know the plans I have for you, declares the Lord, plans to prosper you and not to harm you, plans to give you hope and a future."*

Continuing in this ministry ten years, I heard stories consisting of physical, emotional, sexual and spiritual abuse. There were stories of trauma and abuse worse than mine and less than mine in detail. One time, I remember a woman sharing her story and I found myself holding my breath. It felt like I couldn't breathe, it was unfathomable people could harm their children, sexually and spiritually. It taught me and I share with you, never minimize someone's pain including your own. There were times in group sessions, as I state before, I felt like I was walking on holy ground. I recall another woman who had remained quiet most of the group sessions and had not shared her own story. She came to a session about half way through the group, that session she began to pour out her heart. She was definitely listening and learning through the group sessions. All that time she was thinking and absorbing. We gained her trust and she shared her story. It takes courage to look at what happened, to dig through all the garbage of confused feelings and allow others to walk with you. The process leads to God's healing and better relationship with God, yourself and others.

Open Hearts Ministry was such a blessing to my life and I am so grateful. I learned from every group I participated in or facilitated. Now, I am not actively leading groups. However, being a part of the ministry, I gained dear close friends, who continue to feed into my life and I into theirs. We know each other from the inside out and there is no pretense. God still sends people my way from a variety of encounters who have been broken. I can share my story along with my experience, strength and hope; along with directing them to a healing Group for help and support.

People who are traumatized by sexual abuse can respond differently to the trauma. The Open Hearts Ministry curriculum outlines roles we adopt to cope. For example, I took the role of a "good girl" wanting to do everything right, working hard to please, a people pleaser and never getting into trouble. My sister dealt with her abuse by acting out and tried to run away from it. I believe we both needed the same things, safe environment, love, acceptance and understanding. Our personalities were different, and we differed in the coping skills developed to survive the abuse.

I believe, if I had not dealt with my past, the past would continue to cloud my life and keep me locked up inside an emotional prison. Living in the past and believing lies I had concluded about myself, brought me more fear and pain. Challenging those lies intellectually and seeking to grow spiritually, both in knowledge of God and the wisdom of His word, healed my heart and emotions. In the present, I can visit the past for understanding, but I don't live there anymore.

CHAPTER XI

Church and Community

What is the church? No church is perfect, as it is filled with imperfect human beings. I am one of those imperfect human beings. If there were a perfect church, the minute I attend it would become imperfect. I have accepted myself as a sinner saved by God's grace. My humanity gets the best of me at times. I am capable of being selfish, insensitive, saying the wrong thing and I make mistakes. However, being a Christian, I know I am a worthy child of God and have no need to feel worthless, if God accepts me should I not accept myself? Once I confess a wrong, I know to turn around (repent) and ask God for forgiveness. With assurance of forgiveness, I am restored through Christ's sacrifice for me. Church is not a building, an organization nor denomination. To me, church should be a community of believers gathering to learn, and to grow spiritually as a Christ follower. The church, I believe, has a mission established in God's word to carry the good news of Jesus Christ. The message I received from that good news is one of hope, love, forgiveness and peace. Grounded in my faith, I am free to love without condemnation. Simply, in the book of Matthew18:19 (ESV), Jesus' words are "where two or three gather in my name, there am I with them."

In my opinion, religion, rules and operating procedures are man-made. While an organized church must have structure for functioning in the community, it should not be more important than my individual personal relationship with God. In my decision to join church, I wanted a place to worship and grow spiritually in the knowledge of God. Also, I was seeking evidence of acceptance and genuine caring. God is love. In these days and times of much turmoil and division, I want my church to teach the truth from God's inspired and authoritative word in the Bible. I also want my church's door to be open to all and God's grace, not condemnation, be extended through loving relationships. As a Christian, my words and actions in approaching non-believers should always be prayed about seeking God's will before I speak or act. I pray my behavior and actions will draw people to Christ not push them away. The Apostle Paul states in scripture, Romans 8:1-2 (NIV) *"Therefore, there is now no condemnation for those who are in Christ Jesus because through Christ Jesus the law of the Spirit who gives life has set you free from the law of sin and death."* Folks, through my journey to faith, this says to me pure and simply "it is LOVE that transforms life NOT condemnation."

It is 2022 and the political landscape is so divisive. Reflecting and pondering the news today, I don't see a lot of LOVE. News is filled with hateful things said by and to people in all levels of government, society and even in churches. The questions I ask myself are; "How do I love others honestly in ways that draws them to God, not away?" and How do I respond in love, especially to those with whom I disagree or don't like?" One scripture that helps me in relationship to others is Psalm 19:14 (ESV) "May these words of my mouth and this meditation of my heart be pleasing in your sight, Lord, my Rock and Redeemer." If I pray for God's words and His will (way) before I approach someone, then I will be empowered by God's grace to speak in LOVE…. LOVE is the answer. By seeking God's direction and following Jesus' example we can learn to love others in all circumstances good or bad. God transforms hearts through love, one at a time.

Romans 12:2

*Do not conform to the pattern of this world, but be transformed by the **renewing** of your **mind**. Then you will be able to test and approve what God's will is—his good, pleasing and perfect will.*

Isaiah 61:1-3

*"The Spirit of the Sovereign Lord is on me, because the Lord has anointed me to proclaim good news to the poor. He has sent me to bind up the brokenhearted, to proclaim freedom for the captives and release from the darkness for the prisoners, to proclaim the year of the Lord's favor and the day of vengeance of our God, to comfort all who mourn, and provide for those who grieve in Zion— to bestow on them a crown of beauty instead of **ashes**, the oil of joy instead of mourning, and a garment of praise instead of a spirit of despair. They will be called oaks of righteousness, a planting of the LORD for the display of his splendor."*

CHAPTER XII

Forgiveness

Forgiveness is necessary to personal healing. However, I could not truly forgive until I learned of the harm or poison the abuser dumped into my life. That is why, I have chosen to write about forgiveness toward the end of this book. To understand forgiveness and how important it is to personal healing, I had to learn what forgiveness is not. The following are statements of what I have come to know.

- Forgiveness is not a feeling.
  - "Forgiveness is for me, a releasing of my anger and resentment toward my parents.
- Forgiveness is not pretending or condoning behavior.
  - My mom and dad hurt me. My mom was in denial and did not support me when I told the truth. My life was negatively affected by my dad's sexual abuse and my mom's denial.
- Forgiveness doesn't mean you trust the offender or restore relationship with them.
  - If the abuser is remorseful and getting help to change their behavior, then maybe after a substantial period of sustained change in behavior, a relationship may be possible. I forgave my dad and Mom but my relationship with them was guarded, lacked trust and openness.

- Forgiveness does not relieve the abuser of their responsibility.
  - I forgave my dad and mom, however, that doesn't excuse their behavior. They were the adults and I was the child.

Forgiveness gave me freedom to love without putting my expectations on others. Forgiveness was only possible through my faith in God. I loved my parents and did not seek revenge in anger. Change in their behavior was up to them. Peace and freedom on my journey grew, as a result of learning how to forgive those who hurt me.

CHAPTER XIII

Life's Journey Continues

Each day I wake up is a gift of life, a "New Day" filled with hope. The beginning of each year is a gift, a "New Year" filled with opportunities to love unconditionally and grow in knowledge and wisdom. Whatever days of life remaining for me, I now know will be filled with a multitude of thoughts and feelings. I am grateful that I now feel equipped to handle both the positive and negative circumstances of my life. Had I not gone on this healing journey and walked through the pain of the past, I would not be in this day feeling most grateful. I have done a lot of things along my healing journey to aid my healing, but it has been my relationship with God where past emotions have been exposed and healed. In the daily circumstances of living, a situation occurs or someone says words that remind me of past wounds or triggers me emotionally, I can overreact and will revisit the past. The difference is, now I revisit the past to learn from it. I don't live in the past anymore; nor do I make choices from the prospective and emotions of the wounded, immature little girl (Lynnie) inside.

I am coming to the end of sharing my journey of healing with you. One day there will be an ending to my physical life, and I will go to my eternal home. Life is filled with both bad and good moments. I do not believe we are meant to live life in isolation. I believe people are the most important of God's creation. I do look forward to my future days, as life continues "One Day at a Time." I pray and hope you see yourself in some words or parts of this book. I desire with all my heart to encourage you in some way. Further, I pray you find a relationship with God the Father. If you are angry and / or have resolved not to believe in God, Jesus or religion; I pray you employ all the tools available to you to seek, understand and accept yourself. I believe that journey of seeking will bring you to truth and freedom. You are on this earth for a unique purpose and your value is priceless. I came to believe that about myself. If I could, for all hurting and wounded people, I would give them a gift wrapped in beautiful paper and tied with extravagant bows. Contained inside the box, would be a healthy self-caring love for self, the capacity to see beyond themselves, the ability to love others unconditionally, and a strong, growing faith in God. These are the things I seek, as I grow in my relationship with God, I cannot do them on my own.

> *"God, open the ears, mind and heart of anyone who reads this book. As I prayed for your words and direction in writing, I ask that it is a blessing in some way to every reader. Thank you for your grace and help in each and every day of my life."*

CHAPTER XIV

Closing and Final Thoughts

A s I close and offer final thoughts, I would like to l leave you with a beautiful story, author unknown, that illustrates how we don't have power to alleviate others' sufferings. We have great God-given power to change our own behavior and lives, but there are times we cannot control what happens to us. However, we can learn to love ourselves and others in healthy and whole ways and leave the transformation to God.

The Butterfly Story

Once upon a time in a land far far away.
There was a wonderful old man who loved everything.
Animals, spiders, insects......
One day while walking through the woods
the nice old man found a cocoon.
Feeling lonely he decided to take the cocoon home
to watch its beautiful transformation from a funny
little cocoon to a beautiful butterfly.
He gently placed the cocoon on his kitchen
table, and watched over it for days.
Suddenly on the seventh day the cocoon started to move.
It moved frantically! The old man felt sorry for
the little butterfly inside the cocoon.

He watched it struggle and struggle and struggle!
Finally, the old man feeling so sorry for the cocooned
butterfly rushed to its side with a surgical scalpel and
gently slit the cocoon so the butterfly could emerge.
Just one slice was all it took, and the butterfly broke free from
its cocoon only to wilt over in a completely motionless state.
Well, he felt so sorry for the little creature that he
decided the best thing he could do for the butterfly
was to place it gently back into its cocoon.
He did so, and placed a drop of honey on it to seal the cocoon,
leaving the butterfly to nestle in its natural state. Well, the
next day he noticed that the cocoon was moving again.
Wow, he said! It moved and moved and struggled and struggled.
Finally, the butterfly broke free from its cocoon
and stretched its wings out far and wide.
Big time yawn! Its so beautiful wings were
filled with wonderful colors!
It looked around and took off!
It was flying! It's so beautiful!
The old man was jumping with joy! Wow!
Well from then on, the old man knew that loving something
sometimes means to pray for it and cheer it up!
He realized that God was wonderful, and that sometimes
appearances aren't what they seem to be.
That we all are beautiful butterflies, even though
we have our apparent struggles in life.....

Author Unknown

Like the butterfly, I had to struggle while inside my cocoon of isolation and emotional pain. Some thoughts to share that I have come to believe, as my journey continues in this day.

- You <u>can</u> live your life free of the past, it does take commitment and openness to change. A willingness to look within honestly, not to put down but to learn from.
- Let go of pride, be humble and admit you may need help, which could be as simple as exposing secrets and talking to a trusted pastor, teacher or friend.
- You nor I have all the answers! Your intellect and knowledge will help you learn but it will be wisdom that instructs your reality in loving and living. I pray your journey leads you to God, as I believe wisdom comes from God. We need to know our feelings and emotions, but not live by them. I believe feelings and emotions are part of God's creation to instruct us about ourselves. From feelings, we learn what our needs are and what motives we may have in acting. If I listen to the small still voice of the Holy Spirit of Christ living in me, it will help me in making a choice or taking an action.
- It is true, I am and you are a unique beautiful person worthy of love, care and of immense value. God has given me freedom to choose and make needed changes in my life. I believe God gave each of us the power of free choice.
- As the lyrics of a song sung by Lee Ann Womack states, "Promise me you'll give faith a fighting chance, and when you get the choice to sit it out or dance. I hope you dance.... I hope you dance."

Every day is new. Every January 1st starts a new year. We can have new life; the choice is ours. Enjoy the journey and remember the beautiful butterfly in your living!!!!

With love, prayers and peace,

Linda Kay
Author

REFERENCES, INFORMATION AND PERSONAL THOUGHTS

ALCOHOLISM

Alcoholics Anonymous (AA): On the AA website, https://www. aa.org/what-is-aa, you will see a selection labeled "About AA", which states

> *"Alcoholics Anonymous is a fellowship of people who come together to solve their drinking problem. It doesn't cost anything to attend A.A. meetings. There are no age or education requirements to participate. Membership is open to anyone who wants to do something about their drinking problem. AA.'s primary purpose is to help alcoholics to achieve sobriety.*

On the website, you can enter your city and state for information about local AA organizations. You can obtain contact information and where meetings are held in your area. You will also find a lot of resources, educational information and self-evaluation tools. These tools and information may answer questions you have, and help you understand what is happening in your life.

If you don't have access to a personal computer, you may gain access to a computer or receive information and/or help by:

- Contacting your local county, city or state community health department.
- Access a computer at your local library.
- Counseling and mental health agencies and organizations.
- Larger churches may have separate counseling staff, who can help with counseling and/or provide information.
- There are churches where AA meetings are held, not all churches embrace AA.

Al-Anon & Alateen: Al-Anon is for adults and Alateen is for children and teenagers. The online Al-Anon website at https://al-anon.org/ has a lot of educational information and resources. Both Al-Anon and Alateen are programs to help the family members whose lives are affected by a loved one's alcoholism. You can also find local meeting information by typing in your city and state. Taken from the website, here is a short explanation of the programs and who goes to Al-Anon or Alateen.

> *"Al-Anon members are people, just like you, who are worried about someone with a drinking problem.*
>
> *In Al-Anon and Alateen, members share their own experience, strength, and hope with each other. You will meet others who share your feelings and frustrations, if not your exact situation. We come together to learn a better way of life, to find happiness whether the alcoholic is still drinking or not."*

If you don't have access or regularly use computers for online information, you can:

- Contact your local county, city or state community health department.
- Access information or use a computer at your local library.

- Counseling and mental health agencies will have information.
- Church pastors and those larger churches, who have a counseling staff, often can help and/or provide information. Be aware that some churches hold AA and/or Al-Anon meetings on their premises, but there are churches that do not embrace AA or Al-Anon.
- Contact your local AA organization, sometimes community resources know about AA but not Al-Anon. Local AA organizations and meetings usually know about Al-Anon and Alateen.

"The Lois Wilson Story: When Love Is Not Enough": This is a powerful movie telling what it was like for Lois Wilson, the wife of AA Co-founder, Bill Wilson. Lois is the founder of Al-Anon. The movie is available and can be purchased online, just do an online search using the title. At one time, I know you could buy it on Amazon. You may also be able to get it at your local library and, and if you have a smart TV, some streaming services have the movie free of cost. I think one anonymous reviewer's comment sums up the value of the movie by saying, "This movie helped me come to terms with a loved one's alcoholism. Very inspiring and truthful!"

Sexual, Physical, Mental and Spiritual Abuse

Open Hearts Ministry (ohm): The website is https://ohmin.org/ where you will find statements regarding their values and mission, along with a lot of educational information and resources for personal healing. The organization oversees printed materials used in the Journey Groups, including curriculum. They design, coordinate and plan training for group leaders. You will find an online form, at their website, to fill out and find a registered group in your area. Talk to your local church care ministers about the training and beginning such a group in your local church.

Journey Groups are usually held in area churches and can go by different names i.e., Healing Hearts or Open Hearts. I would suggest you make sure their curriculum is from Open Hearts Ministry. The curriculum has continued to develop, be updated and now is time-tested in experience, to facilitate healing from the effects of trauma and abuse.

A journey group, usually consists of two trained leaders (training means they have attended Open Hearts Ministry training and have been participants in two journey groups themselves.) Each group will meet for 9 or 12 sessions and participants will be kept at 6-10 members. Leaders will facilitate discussion with participants. Everyone, including leaders, are to agree upon a written confidentiality agreement and rules for safety and trustworthiness. Participants can leave the group at any time, however, to build trust a group is considered closed to new members after the first or second week.

Becoming a group leader is a personal choice, and not all participants become leaders. I am so grateful to having been a leader for 10 years. During the time I led groups, my understanding of myself and others grew so much. Being involved in the ministry gave me a lifetime gift, the gift of making "heart" friends who love, accept, support and encourage me, just as I am.

Here are statements from the Open Hearts Ministry website:

"Life is a path marked by hurt, hope and struggles.

*At Open Hearts, we train you to engage people along that **journey** in deeper and healthier ways.*

*Through a safe and confidential group process, our curriculum leads you through your own **stories** of pain, disappointment and abuse, equipping you to share the care you receive with others. We teach you to share and listen honestly. We show you how to* *practice good self-care. We seek to love like Jesus, with empathy and forgiveness. We help you create authentic community where people are heard, loved and **healed together**."*

PROFESSIONAL HELP

PSCHIATRISTS, PSYCHOLOGISTS AND COUNSELING AGENCIES: You can find resources online, and at your local mental health department, (county, city or state) health departments, church pastors or care ministries, libraries and through others who have had experience with counseling professionals. You can check credentials (education and licensing) through your local or state's regulatory agencies.

In my experience, and as a suggestion to you, begin trusting yourself even if you cannot yet trust others. If you begin counseling and something feels or seems strange to you or unsafe, maybe you need a different professional working with you?

Here are some tips I found to be true:

> *A GOOD counseling professional will not give you "answers on how to fix you." They will listen and help you discover your true feelings, what changes or boundaries you need to set, or what emotional needs you might have; in order for you to find healthier ways to cope with life. They will give you factual and educational information. Also, they will hold you accountable to the goals you set for yourself.*

If you cannot afford mental health services, local churches and service organizations may be able to help. Some larger churches can have counselors on staff who are trained and licensed and can provide counseling for free or reduced fees. Christian counseling organizations sometimes offer an "ability to pay" fee schedule. Just don't give up, if funds are the issue, look within your community for emotional and financial help.

Psychiatrists usually are involved when you have a mental health diagnosis for which you need medication. Medication can be prescribed temporarily and for a period of time while you are regularly counseling. Medications can be prescribed for long-term use in the case of mental health disease like Bi-polar etc. If you are seeing a psychiatrist, make sure they know other medications and diseases affecting you. Be honest with them about yourself, this is paramount to you getting the best care. Doctors can only help, if they have all the facts. You can give them permission to coordinate with your primary medical doctor. Your medical doctor may have the best physical history of your past surgeries, current medications and/or diseases affecting you.

BOOKS AND MATERIALS

Looking backwards and moving forward, I feel so richly blessed by authors, pastors, teachers and professionals who have written books and materials which have helped me and others. Of course, I cannot mention all the books, nor all the online and written materials, which helped me. So, I selected those most instrumental in helping me heal early on my journey. Be open, and seek learning. I know God will guide you to people, books, movies, songs and materials which speak to your heart and mind. Also, if you have a disability, there are audio books and books in braille.

One Day at A Time in Al-Anon: This daily meditation book is printed by Al-Anon Family Group Organization and can be ordered online, or purchased at some local Al-Anon meetings. All meditations are written by Al-Anon members whose names are anonymous. Al-Anon members use only first names in meetings, and remain anonymous publicly. This book is also printed in other languages.

Recently, I again read the introduction to this book, as if it was the first time. The book I read from is the tenth printing, 1973 (ISBN-0-910034-16-8). There will be newer versions, however, it is still a book for anyone, regardless of race or culture. A quote from the introduction:

> *"Mindful of the fact that the Al-Anon fellowship*
> *embraces people of many lands, creeds and customs,*

the book avoids, so far as possible, identification with those of the United States where Al-Anon happened to have had its beginning. These daily messages are intended for all people, all ways of life."

My book is approximately 45 years old and held together with gray colored duct tape. Within its' pages, are many hand written notes about things I want to remember. These printed pages, along with my written notes, hold such great wisdom I heard from so many people. People I learned from, and who had walked the road of healing from the effects of alcoholism. "I suppose I should at some point get a new one, but why? The book, with all my notes, feels like an old friend in my hand. A friend for whom I give God thanks."

"When Trust is Lost; Healing for Victims of Sexual Abuse": This booklet was copyrighted in 1992 and is available through RBC Ministries at http://www.rbc.org . This ministry also prints "Our Daily Bread", which is a daily devotional booklet and is available free at restaurants, and other public places. You usually see it at the entrance with other pamphlets or by the cashier. I don't remember when or where I picked up my copy of this booklet. I do know, it was early in the beginning of my healing journey. Over the years, I have asked for copies of this booklet, as it impacted me in a way that helped me understand and feel understood. I have taken it to church welcome centers, and given it out to others struggling with childhood sexual abuse (incest). I recently called to order more copies, thinking it would no longer be available or surely had been revised, but was told it had not changed over those years. The booklet remains the same, as when it was originally written, I think due to the information and wisdom within its pages. The author is Dr. Dan B. Allender, a Christian Psychologist who was abused as a child. In my opinion, the booklet outlines the problems an abuse victim (child) experiences and what the healing steps look like. This booklet, I can't state this enough, gave me such understanding and I felt so understood. A couple quotes from initial pages:

"Sexual abuse is one of the few crimes that brings more shame to the victim than to the offender."

"The pain of understanding and healing is far less than the pain of denial and despair"

<u>The Wounded Heart</u>: This book was authored by Dr. Dan B. Allender, and was the first book, I found early 1980's in the public library on the subject of incest and sexual abuse. Currently, there are lots of books written on the subject in your public library. However, in the 1980's, I didn't find many books on the subject in the library. The book does get somewhat academic, at times, but I encourage you to stick with it to learn and understand about yourself. You can break it down into small bits, by reading a topical section and pondering it for a while. Depending on where you are in your own "healing journey", you may not want to sit down and read it front to back? That could be overwhelming, confusing or just too much to take in. For quick reference and understanding, check out the back of the book you will find quick sections offering "Notes" (which outlines the chapters), "About the Author" and "Resources for Inner Change". The "Prologue: The Quest for a Cure" contains the following from Dr. Allender's experience with his daughter.

"My eight-year-old daughter once asked me, "Daddy, why are you interested in sexual abuse?" Thankfully, before I could answer she asked another question: "Daddy, do abused people have walls in their hearts that keep them from being happy, and will they have less bricks in their walls after reading your book?" I wept. Her simple questions expressed the heart of my personal calling (why I am interested in abuse?) and

my professional task (will this book help?) and opened the door to deep gratitude."

The Wounded Heart addresses sexual abuse from the spiritual sense of who we are in God. Not everyone dealing with this issue, has had a good experience when contacting a church, a pastor or another Christian believer for help. Through the contact, they may have been rejected or given words that led them to believe it was all their fault. The first thing to state to a survivor is "it is not your fault." Doing otherwise, can move them emotionally into deeper shame and confusion. Feeling shameful, confused and/or bad about myself moved me into coping mechanisms of hiding and numbing of feelings. That coping strategy in defining myself kept me angry and cut off from the presence of God. This led me to anger, distance, mistrust and, for a while, I rejected God.

The effects of sexual abuse had deposited confusion, anger and hurt feelings into my heart and soul. God led me through that "personal mine field" and into the light, even when I didn't acknowledge him. It was years later; I began to have personal relationship. My eyes were opened to his grace, which had been there all along. Don't encumber yourself or limit yourself with timelines. If someone or anyone in trying to assist you causes you to feel like sexual abuse is your fault, question whether this relationship or professional is ok for you. Please trust yourself, as I believe with all my heart, God is in the details of healing and will lead. You can trust him as the ultimate healer. You can come to trust yourself in your healing journey. Through seeking and learning, I pray, you will come to trust yourself and to see God's presence on your journey.

<u>*A Case for Christ:*</u> A book written by Lee Strobel, formerly an atheist and a Journalist for Chicago Tribune. In this book he outlines his investigation into whether Christ existed or not, he lays it out in an investigative and clear, logical way. It is his personal story of how his investigation led him without a doubt from atheism to Christianity.

A statement from an anonymous reviewer of the book. "The facts are substantial, the interviews (with their lengthy credentials) informative and thought provoking, the overall compilation of this book, told in a compelling narrative, make this a great read for skeptics and Christians alike."

Lee Strobel says of the experience of writing the book this quote "My conversion is a deeply personal experience that changed my life and the course I was currently on."

Printed in the United States
by Baker & Taylor Publisher Services